1990
Traveler's Guide to Museum Exhibitions

Museum Guide Publications, Inc.

Front Cover:

Surf, Nantasket, c. 1900–05, by Maurice Brazil Prendergast. Courtesy of Williams College Museum of Art, Williamstown, Mass.; gift of Mrs. Charles Prendergast.

Chosen in honor of the 1990 traveling exhibition, *The Art of Maurice Brazil Prendergast,* organized by the Williams College Museum of Art, and traveling to the Whitney Museum of American Art (May 31–Sept. 2), Williams College Museum of Art (Oct. 6–Dec. 16), Los Angeles County Museum of Art (Feb. 21–Apr. 22, 1991), The Phillips Collection (May 18–Aug. 25, 1991).

Photo Credits:

Ray Andrews, 36
E. Irving Blomstrann, 90
Michael Bodycomb, 43
Geoffrey Clements, 85
Richard Eells, 68
Hickey & Robertson, Houston, 59
H. Korol, 142
Rollyn Puterbaugh, 32
Jon Reis, 53
Joseph Szaszfai, 46, 73
Patrick J. Young, 45

Copyright © 1990 by Museum Guide Publications, Inc., P.O. Box 25369, 1619 31st Street, N.W., Washington, D.C. 20007. No part of this guide may be reproduced without the publisher's permission. Produced by Ripinsky & Company. Distributed by Grove Weidenfeld, 841 Broadway, New York, New York 10003-4793.

ISBN 1-55584-451-0   ISSN 1041-0724

Table of Contents

Foreword, Acknowledgements	iv
Traveling Exhibition Sampler	v
U.S. Museum Entries, by city	1
Museums of Canada, by province	141
Color Portfolio	after 74
Index by museum	151
by state	152
Reorder coupon	153

Introduction

The **1990 Traveler's Guide to Museum Exhibitions** welcomes museums of Canada, and several additional U.S. museums. An expanded Traveling Exhibition Sampler, color portfolio, and an index by state have been added in response to reader requests. Wide margin space is provided for notes.

Asterisks (*) in the guide signify exhibitions organized by or traveling under the auspices of the American Federation of Arts.

Crosses (†) in the guide denote exhibitions represented by a color photograph in the Color Portfolio.

While every effort has been made to ensure accuracy, exhibition dates and hours are subject to change. Please telephone museums to double check information.

What's Inside:

* Traveling Exhibition Sampler
* Color Portfolio
* 1990 Calendars for 107 American and 7 Canadian Museums
* Permanent Collections and Permanent Collection Highlights
* Addresses and Phone Nunbers
* Hours and Admissions
* Tours and Handicapped Facilities
* Refreshment Opportunities
* "Other Collections of Note"
* Index by Museum and State
* Coupon for additional 1990 copies and 1991 reservations

Foreword

It is with great enthusiasm that I applaud the publication of the **1990 Traveler's Guide to Museum Exhibitions**, an indispensable planning guide for everyone involved in the visual arts. I have watched the Guide evolve over the past two years—it is an extraordinarily inventive publication, and it is hard to believe that such a guide didn't exist before Susan Rappaport compiled this information. There is indeed a need for a handy guide that will inform museum goers about annual traveling exhibitions and where and when they can be seen. The **Traveler's Guide** is eminently useful for artists, travelers, and all appreciators of excellence in art. It also provides a permanent record of exhibitions—a fine resource for the scholar and the lay person. Most importantly, the **Traveler's Guide** shows how museums are flourishing, how they grow and change from year to year, and how vital creative expression and imaginative spirit are to our lives.

Livingston Biddle
> *Author of <u>Our Government and the Arts</u>, former Chairman of the National Endowment for the Arts.*

Acknowledgements

I again thank museum staff for their interest and speedy responses to requests for the information, which keeps the guide up-to-date. I also thank Jessica Beels, and the Associate Editor, Nicole De Lisle, who brought to the guide her expertise in graphics and book design.

Susan S. Rappaport, *Editor and Publisher*

1990 Traveling Exhibition Sampler

Albert Pinkham Ryder
National Museum of American Art (Apr. 6–July 29), The Brooklyn Museum (Sept. 21–Jan. 8, 1991).

†Bay Area Figurative Art, 1950–1965
San Francisco Museum of Modern Art (thru Feb. 4), Hirshhorn Museum and Sculpture Garden (June 13–Sept. 9), Pennsylvania Academy of Fine Arts (Oct. 5–Dec. 30).

Childe Hassam: An Island Garden Revisited
Yale University Art Museum (Apr. 4–June 10), Denver Art Museum (July 4–Sept. 9), National Museum of American Art (Oct. 5–Jan. 6, 1991).

†Czech Modernism: 1900–1945
The Museum of Fine Arts, Houston (thru Jan. 7), The Brooklyn Museum (Mar. 2–May 7).

†Expressionism and Modern German Painting from the Thyssen-Bornemisza Collection
National Gallery of Art (thru Jan. 14), Kimbell Art Museum (Jan. 27–Mar. 25), The Fine Arts Museums of San Francisco (Apr. 18–July 1).

†Francis Bacon
Hirshhorn Museum and Sculpture Garden (thru Jan. 7), Los Angeles County Museum of Art (Feb. 11–Apr. 29), The Museum of Modern Art, New York (May 24–Aug. 28).

From Fontainebleau to the Louvre: French Master Drawings 1600–1650
Cleveland Museum of Art (thru Jan. 28), Harvard Art Museums (Feb. 24–Apr. 8), The National Gallery of Canada (May 4–June 17).

†*Gold of Africa: Jewelry and Ornaments from Ghana, Côte d'Ivoire, Mali, and Senegal
The Metropolitan Museum of Art (thru Mar. 11), Dallas Museum of Art (Apr. 8–June 10), Denver Art Museum (July 21–Sept. 16), Birmingham Museum of Art (Oct. 21–Jan. 2, 1991).

†Helen Frankenthaler: A Paintings Retrospective
Modern Art Museum of Fort Worth (thru Jan. 7), Los Angeles County Museum of Art (Feb. 8–Apr. 22), The Detroit Institute of Arts (June 24–Sept. 2).

*I Dream a World: Portraits of Black Women Who Changed America
Birmingham Museum of Art (Feb. 4–Mar. 11), Denver Art Museum (Apr. 7–June 3), Spencer Museum of Art, (Sept. 23–Nov. 18).

†Impressionism: Selections from Five American Museums
The Minneapolis Institute of Arts (Jan. 28–Mar. 25), The Nelson-Atkins Museum of Art, (Apr. 21–June 17), The Saint Louis Art Museum (July 14–Sept. 9), The Toledo Museum of Art (Sept. 30–Nov. 25).

†**The Intimate Interiors of Edouard Vuillard**
Museum of Fine Arts, Houston (thru Jan. 28), The Phillips Collection (Feb. 17–Apr. 29), The Brooklyn Museum (May 18–July 30).

†**Jim Dine Drawings**
The Minneapolis Institute of Arts (thru Feb. 11), Joslyn Art Museum (Apr. 21–June 24), The Fine Arts Museums of San Francisco (July 29–Oct. 7).

Leaves from the Bodhi Tree: The Art of Pala India
The Dayton Art Institute (thru Jan. 14), Walters Art Gallery (Feb. 10–Apr. 15).

†**Masterpieces of Impressionism and Postimpressionism: The Annenberg Collection**
National Gallery of Art (May 6–Aug. 5), Los Angeles County Museum of Art (Aug. 16–Nov. 4).

Matisse in Morocco
National Gallery of Art (Mar. 18–June 3), The Museum of Modern Art, New York (June 21–Sept. 4).

Monet in the Nineties: The Series Paintings
Museum of Fine Arts, Boston (Feb. 7–Apr. 29), The Art Institute of Chicago (May 19–Aug. 12).

The New Vision: Photography between the World Wars
San Francisco Museum of Modern Art (Mar. 1–Apr. 22), Los Angeles County Museum of Art (May 10–July 15), The Art Institute of Chicago (Sept. 15–Dec. 12).

†**Pierre Bonnard: The Graphic Works**
The Metropolitan Museum of Art (thru Feb. 4), The Museum of Fine Arts, Houston (Feb. 25–Apr. 29), The Museum of Fine Arts, Boston (May 25–July 29).

Robert Mapplethorpe
University Art Museum, Berkeley (Jan. 17–Mar. 18), The Institute of Contemporary Art, Boston (Aug. 1–Sept. 16).

†**The Romance of the Taj Mahal**
Los Angeles County Museum of Art (thru Mar. 11), The Toledo Museum of Art (Apr. 29–June 24), The Virginia Museum of Fine Arts (Aug. 22–Nov. 25).

Yoruba: Nine Centuries of African Art and Thought
The Art Institute of Chicago (Feb. 10–Apr. 1), National Museum of African Art (May 11–Aug. 26), The Cleveland Museum of Art (Oct. 10–Dec. 9).

10 + 10: Contemporary Soviet and American Painting
Albright-Knox Art Gallery (thru Jan. 7), Milwaukee Art Museum (Feb. 2–Mar. 25), Corcoran Gallery of Art (Apr. 21–June 24).

Atlanta, Ga.

The High Museum of Art

1280 Peachtree St. N.E., Atlanta, Ga. 30309
(404) 892-HIGH (recorded)

1990 Exhibitions
Thu Jan. 14
Art in Berlin, 1815–1989
Examines the way artists have responded to the social changes that have shaped Berlin; includes work by Beckmann, Kirchner, Liebermann, Lissitsky, Menzel, Moholy-Nagy, Munch. Catalogue.

Feb. 20–Apr. 15
Art at the Edge: Daniel Reeves
Presentation of "The Well of Patience," the first video installation by this acclaimed New York artist. Catalogue.

Feb. 20–May 6
Treasures from the Fitzwilliam Museum
Chosen from the extensive collection of the Fitzwilliam Museum of Cambridge University; includes paintings by Delacroix, Hals, Hogarth, Monet, Rubens, Titian, Van Dyke. Catalogue.

May 22–Aug. 5
Black Art–Ancestral Legacy
Explores African cultural roots in black visual arts in the U.S. and the Caribbean during the last 50 years. Catalogue.

Aug. 1–Oct. 14
Max Weber: The Cubist Years
The first comprehensive examination of Weber's work, 1910–20; includes paintings of figures, performers, and cities. Catalogue.

Aug. 28–Nov. 11
New Discoveries in Georgia's Decorative Arts
Catalogue.

Oct. 16–Dec. 9
Art at the Edge
The seventh exhibition in a series on contemporary artists. Catalogue.

Oct. 30–Jan. 20
Constructed Images: New Photography
Sixty images by Eda, Georgiou, Karp, Rodriquez, Simpson, Sligh, Walker, and others. Catalogue.

Three Up, Three Down, 1973, by Alexander Calder. The High Museum of Art; loan from Calder's estate and The Pace Gallery, N.Y.

Permanent Collection
European painting and sculpture from the Renaissance to the 20th century; Sub-Saharan African art; American and European prints, photographs, decorative arts; American 18th- to 20th-century paintings and sculptures. **Highlights:** Lichtenstein, *Sandwich and Soda;* Peale, *Senator William H.*

Austin, Tex.

Crawford of Georgia; Prendergast, *Procession, Venice;* Rauschenberg, *Overcast III;* Stella, *Manteneia I;* Whittredge, *Landscape in the Harz Mountains.*
Architecture: 1983 building by Meier.

Admission
Adults $4; seniors & students with ID $2; students, 6–17, $1; children under 6 free. Thurs., 1–5, free. Handicapped accessible.

Hours
Tues. & Thurs.–Sat., 10–5; Wed., 10–9; Sun., noon–5. Closed Mon. & holidays.

Tours
Available Sept.–May, Tues.–Sun. Call (404) 898-1145.

Food & Drink
Pentimento Café (Woodruff Arts Center): Open daily 11:30–2; 6–8.

Laguna Gloria Art Museum
**P.O. Box 5568
3809 West 35th St., Austin, Tex. 78763
(512) 478-8191**

1990 Exhibitions
Thru Jan. 21
First Impressions: Early Prints by Forty-six Contemporary Artists
Focuses on prints by leading American artists including Dine, Johns, Rauschenberg, Warhol. Catalogue.

Jan. 27–Mar. 4
Peter Saul
Retrospective of the contemporary Austin artist's work.

Mar. 10–Apr. 29
Feathers, Fur, and Fins
Incorporates animal representations in a variety of media by Texas artists. Includes a children's hands-on gallery.

June 9–July 29
Thomas Hart Benton: Works on Paper
Drawings, sketches, studies, and 15 associated paintings by one of America's most noted artists.

Aug. 4–Sept. 2
At the Edge: A National Print and Drawing Exhibition

Permanent Collection
The museum presents changing exhibitions of 20th-century American art. Objects from the small collection are not on

Baltimore, Md.

permanent exhibit. Outdoor sculpture from the permanent collection is displayed on the grounds. **Architecture:** 1916 historic landmark Mediterranean-style villa by Page; 1991 building by Venturi planned.

Admission
Adults $2; seniors & students $1; children under 16 free. Thurs., 5–9, free.

Hours
Tues.–Sat.,10–5; Thurs., 10–9; Sun., 1–5. Closed Mon. & holidays.

Tours
Sun. at 2; Mon.–Fri. by reservation. Call (512) 458-8191 or 478-7742.

The Baltimore Museum of Art

Art Museum Dr., Baltimore, Md. 21218
(301) 396-7101; 396-7100 (recorded)

1990 Exhibitions
Thru Jan. 28
Daumier and the Art of Caricature

Thru Jan. 28
"Toys in the Attic": Antique Playthings from the Lawrence Scripps Wilkinson Collection/The Detroit Historical Museum.
Features over 200 toys reflecting changes on the American scene from the mid-19th century to the present.

Thru Feb. 4
*Objects of Bright Pride: Northwest Coast Indian Art from the American Museum of Natural History
Primarily 19th-century objects created by the Bella Bella, Haida, Kwakiutl, Tlingit, and other tribes. Catalogue.

Thru Feb. 18
Drawing Now: Elen Phelan
Thirty drawings of dolls from the artist's extensive collection.

Thru Mar. 18
Baltimore Album Quilts
In celebration of the museum's 75th anniversary, album quilts popular during the mid-19th century are displayed.

Jan. 21–Mar. 11
Roland Freeman: The Arabbers of Baltimore
A prominent African-American photographer documents street vendors who sold produce from horse-drawn carts.

Baltimore, Md.

Feb. 27–Apr. 22
First Impressions: Early Prints by Forty-six Contemporary Artists
Focuses on prints by leading American artists including Dine, Johns, Rauschenberg, Warhol. Catalogue.

Feb. 27–Apr. 29
BMA Collects: Surrealist Drawings
About 30 surrealist and dadaist works by Ernst, Matta, Miró, Tanguy, and others.

Apr. 3–July 1
BMA Collects: Recent Accessions in the Decorative Arts
A variety of objects in various media from different time periods, including American furniture, English and American silver, ceramics, glass, textiles.

Apr. 3–July 22
Fans
Displays 18th- and 19th-century folding fans of various materials and decorative styles.

May 8–June 17
BMA Collects: Drawings from the Thomas E. Benesch Memorial Collection
A selection from the 120 works collected by Vivian and Edward Benesch in memory of their son. Includes drawings by Dine, Johns, Kelly, Rauschenberg.

May 27–July 22
Baltimore Collects: Painting & Sculpture since 1960
Works from local private collections by artists Gilbert & George, de Kooning, LeWitt, Louis, Murray, Puryear.

American Baroque, 1929, by Ralph Steiner. The Baltimore Museum of Art.

June 23–Aug. 5
Rowlandson: Drawings and Watercolors
Features 80 works by the popular Georgian period English artist renowned as an acerbic social commentator. Includes hunting, boxing, racing, and courting scenes as well as landscapes and portraits. Catalogue.

June 26–Aug. 26
Stitching Memories: African-American Story Quilts
Works by both professional and untrained quilters, including Baltimore artists Elizabeth and Joyce Scott.

Permanent Collection
Paintings, sculptures, prints, photographs, drawings; period rooms from 19th-century Maryland houses; Asian, African, Pre-Columbian, Native American, Oceanic art. White Collection of Maryland silver; Cheney Miniature Rooms; Syrian mosaics from Antioch; sculpture gardens.
Highlights: Cone collection of postimpressionist works; Cézanne, *Mont Sainte-Victoire Seen from the Bibemus Quarry;* van Gogh's *A Pair of Boots;* Matisse, *Large Reclining Nude* and *Purple Robe and Anemones;* Picasso, *Dr. Claribel Cone* and *La Coiffure;* Pollock, *Water Birds;*

Baltimore, Md.

Raphael, *Emilia Pia da Montefeltre;* Rembrandt, *Titus;* Van Dyck, *Rinaldo and Armida;* West, *Self-Portrait.*
Architecture: 1929 building and 1937 addition by Pope; 1982 wing and 1986 addition by Bowers, Lewis, and Thrower; 1988 Levi Sculpture Garden by Sasaki Associates.

Admission
Adults $3; full-time students & seniors $2; age 18 & under free. Thurs., free. Handicapped accessible; wheelchairs available.

Hours
Tues.–Fri., 10–4; Thurs., 10–9; Sat.–Sun., 11–6. Closed Mon., Jan. 1, Good Friday, July 4, Thanksgiving, Dec. 25.

Tours
Call (301) 396-6320 for information.

Food & Drink
Museum Café: Tues.–Wed., 11–9; Thurs.–Sat., 11–10; Sun., 11–8. For reservations, call (301) 235-3930.

The Walters Art Gallery

**600 North Charles St., Baltimore, Md. 21201-5185
(301) 547-9000; 547-ARTS (recorded)**

1990 Exhibitions
Thru Jan. 7
Splendor of the Popes: Treasures from the Sistine Chapel and the Vatican Museums and Library
Includes goldsmithwork, illuminated manuscripts, vestments, two tapestries by Raphael, and the 9th-century enamel cross of Pope Paschal I.

Thru Jan. 21
Japanese Cloisonné Enamels: The Fisher Collection
Features enamel or "shippo" work by masters such as Sosuke and Yasuyuki.

Jan. 2–Apr. 1
From Romanesque to Gothic: Illumination in Transition
Examines the dramatic changes of illumination during the form's short practice.

Feb. 18–Apr. 15
Leaves from the Bodhi Tree: The Art of Pala India
First major national exhibition of 250 objects from the Pala dynasty (8th–12th cent.). Catalogue.

Apr. 3–July 1
The Book in the Book: Representations of the Scroll, the Roll, and the Codex in Illuminated Manuscripts

Baltimore, Md.

May 27–July 29
Illuminations: Images of Landscape in France, 1855–1885
Paintings and works on paper by Barbizon and impressionist masters illustrate the evolution of landscape styles. Catalogue.

July 3–Sept. 30
Flemish Illumination in the Fifteenth Century: High Art in the Lowlands
Works by Master of Guillebert de Metz, Master of the Ghent Privileges, Masters of the Gold Scrolls, and later-century artists Liedet, Marmion, and Vrelant.

Sept. 9–Oct. 28
Irish Decorative Arts from the National Museum of Ireland
Features glass, silver, textiles, and small-scale furniture of the Celtic world. Catalogue.

Oct. 2–Dec. 30
The Gothic Revival: The Illuminated Manuscript in Medieval and Modern Times
Displays calligraphy, how-to books, missal-paintings, and paint boxes as well as chromolithographic facsimiles and illustrated histories of the art and culture of the Middle Ages.

Dec. 9–Feb. 17, 1991
Islamic Art and Patronage: Masterpieces from the Kuwait National Museum
Presents a collection of ceramics, gems, jewelry, manuscripts, metalwork, woodwork, and textiles. Catalogue.

Permanent Collection
Antiquities of Egypt and the ancient Near East; Asian, Greek, Etruscan, Roman art; Early Christian and Byzantine art; medieval art of Western Europe; Islamic art; illuminated manuscripts; 16th- to 19th-century paintings, sculptures, prints; Renaissance enamels and jewelry. **Highlights:** Bellini, *Madonna and Child Enthroned with Saints;* Fabergé Easter eggs from the Russian imperial collection; Géricault, *Riderless Racers at Home;* Manet, *At the Café;* Raphael, *Virgin of the Candelabra;* van der Goes, *Portrait of an Unknown Man.* **Architecture:** 1904 Renaissance-revival building by Adams and Delano; courtyard modeled after Palazzo Balbi in Genoa, Italy; 1974 wing by Shepley, Bulfinch, Richardson, and Abbott; renovation of adjacent 1850 mansion under construction.

Admission
Adults $3; seniors $2; students with ID & age 18 & under free. Wed., free. Handicapped accessible.

Hours
Tues.–Sun., 11–5. Closed Mon. & holidays.

Tours
Wed. at 12:30; Sun. at 2. Call (301) 547-9000, ext. 232, Mon.–Fri., 9–5 for information.

Berkeley, Calif.

Other Collections of Note

**The Peale Museum of the Baltimore City Life Museums, 225 Holliday St., Baltimore, Md. 21202
(301) 396-1149**

University Art Museum

**University of California, 2626 Bancroft Way, Berkeley, Calif. 94720
(415) 642-1207; 642-0808**

1990 Exhibitions
Jan. 10–Mar. 11
Jay De Feo
Displays 50 abstract works on paper in various media including graphite, charcoal, oil, pastel, collage. Catalogue.

Jan. 17–Mar. 18
Robert Mapplethorpe
Focuses on 165 still lifes, nudes, and portraits by the late controversial photographer who challenged the traditions of painting and photography. Catalogue.

Apr. 18–June 24
James Lee Byars: The House of Luck
Includes large-scale paper and fabric works and sculptures in gold, marble, and basalt, representing the artist's interest in philosophy, language, and spirituality. Catalogue.

May 16–June 17
MFA/UCB/1990: Parts I and II
Annual display of works by the students of the UC Berkeley Master of Fine Arts program.

July 11–Sept. 16
Designs for Independent Living

Oct. 3–Jan. 6, 1991
Anxious Visions: Surrealist Art
Thematic display of 130 works from 1924–44 including paintings, sculptures, drawings, and photographs by Arp, Brauner, Dali, Ernst, Giacometti, Magritte, Man Ray, Masson, Matta, Miró, and others. Catalogue.

Permanent Collection
Paintings, photographs, prints, drawings, including 16th- to 19th-century European works by Cézanne, Renoir, Rubens; Asian art; 20th-century works by Bacon, Calder, Frankenthaler, Rothko, Still; Pacific Film Archive. **Highlights:** Borofsky, *Hammering Man;* Hofmann collection and archive; Modersohn-Becker, *Head of Peasant Woman;* Rubens, *The Road to Calvary.* **Architecture:** 1965 building by Ciampi.

Ajitto, 1981, by Robert Mapplethorpe. From *Robert Mapplethorpe* at the University Art Museum, Berkeley, Jan. 17–Mar. 18.

Birmingham, Ala.

Admission
Adults $3; seniors & students $2; CAL students & children under 6 free; Thurs., 11–noon, free.

Hours
Wed.–Sun., 11–5. Closed Mon.–Tues. & holidays.

Tours
For reservations call (415) 642-2403, Mon.–Fri.

Food & Drink
Swallow Restaurant: Wed.–Sat., 11–8; Tues. & Sun., 11–5. Closed Mon.

Birmingham Museum of Art

2000 Eighth Ave. North, Birmingham, Ala. 35203 (205) 254-2566; 254-2565 (recorded)

1990 Exhibitions
Jan. 6–Mar. 4
Focus: Fact or Fiction
Features works in a variety of media by Alabama artists.

Jan. 21–Mar. 26
Summoning of the Souls: Treasures from the Tombs of China
Explores life in Han dynasty China (12th–2d century B.C.) through silks, lacquerware, and wooden tomb figurines excavated at the tomb of the marquis of Dai at Mawangdui in Hunan province. Catalogue.

Feb. 4–Mar. 11
*I Dream a World: Portraits of Black Women Who Changed America
Seventy-five portraits by Pulitzer Prize winning photographer Brian Lanker of Maya Angelou, Shirley Chisholm, Odetta, Rosa Parks, Sarah Vaughn, and others. Catalogue.

Mar. 18–June 30
Portraits of Australians: Photographs of Michael O'Brien

Apr. 15–June 10
The Inspired Dream: Life as Art in Aboriginal Australia
Features rock art to contemporary art from various Aboriginal groups of the Northern territory.

Oct. 21–Jan. 2, 1991
†*Gold of Africa: Jewelry and Ornaments from Ghana, Côte d'Ivoire, Mali, and Senegal
Jewelry and royal regalia primarily made by the Akan-speaking peoples in the 19th and 20th centuries. Catalogue.

Boston, Mass.

Permanent Collection
European and American paintings, sculptures, decorative arts; Asian, African, Pre-Columbian, Native American art; English and American silver. **Highlights:** Beeson collection of Wedgwood; Botero, *Reclining Nude;* Mainardi, *Madonna and Child with Saint John and Three Angels;* Remington bronzes; Sargent, *Lady Helen Vincent, Viscountess d'Abernon;* Stella, *Flin-Flon VI.* **Architecture:** 1959 building by Warren, Knight, and Davis; 1966 and 1974 additions; 1991 building by Barnes planned.

Admission
Free. Handicapped accessible.

Hours
Tues.–Sat., 10–5; Thurs., 10–9; Sun., 1–5. Closed Mon., Jan. 1, Dec. 25.

Tours
Call (205) 254-2571.

Food & Drink
Critic's Room Restaurant: Tues.–Fri., 11:30–2.

The Institute of Contemporary Art

955 Boylston St., Boston, Mass. 02115
(617) 266-5151

1990 Exhibitions
Thru Jan. 7
On the Passage: The Situationist International, 1957–1972
First attempt to document the impact of the Situationist International movement—a philosophical and artistic movement that supported the 1969 Paris revolts. Includes paintings, posters, writings, films, models.

Jan. 19–Mar. 11
Currents–Sophie Calle: A Survey

Mar. 30–May 20
Raul Ruiz and Mary Heilman
A multimedia installation, *The Expulsion of the Moors— A Journey through Spanish History*—by Chilean filmmaker Ruiz; includes 16 video channels and 3 constructed chambers, and the first solo exhibition of cool, abstract and geometric images of fluctuating patterns by Heilman.

June 2–July 15
Diamonds Are Forever: Artists and Writers on Baseball
Features paintings, photographs, and drawings that reflect on baseball as a national inspiration.

Boston, Mass.

Aug. 1–Sept. 16
Robert Mapplethorpe
Focuses on 165 still lifes, nudes, and portraits by the late controversial photographer who challenged the traditions of painting and photography. Catalogue.

Sept. 28–Dec. 2
Between Spring and Summer: Recent Developments in Soviet Painting, Architecture and Film
Features paintings, mixed media objects, films, and architectural drawings. Catalogue.

Permanent Collection
No permanent collection. **Architecture:** 1886 Richardsonian building by Vinal; 1970s facade restored and interior redesigned by Gund.

Admission
Adults $4; students $3; seniors & children under 16 $1.50; Thurs., 5–8, free.

Hours
Wed. & Sun., 11–5; Thurs.–Sat. 11–8. Closed Mon.–Tues. & holidays.

Tours
Call (617) 266-5152.

Isabella Stewart Gardner Museum

280 the Fenway, Boston, Mass. 02115
(617) 566-1401; 734-1359 (recorded)

1990 Exhibitions
Thru Feb. 4
Mrs. Gardner's Circle: Henry James, Francis Marion Crawford, Amy Lowell, and T. S. Eliot
Letters, photographs, and other memorabilia illustrate Mrs. Gardner's relationships with her circle of friends.

Feb. 4–May 13
Amateurs, Professionals, and Kodak Fiends: Portraits and Other Photographs from the Gardner Collection
Includes family daguerreotypes, a diascope viewer with early color images, and portraits from many famous studios and renowned local photographers.

May 15–Sept. 16
Boston's Mrs. Gardner
Focuses on Mrs. Gardner's place in the Boston cultural tradition; her correspondence with eminent Bostonians; and her interest in and support of local arts, institutions, music, and sports.

Boston, Mass.

Permanent Collection
Italian Renaissance paintings; Dutch, French, German, Spanish masterpieces; American paintings; rare books and manuscripts; decorative arts. Works permanently arranged as Mrs. Gardner specified. **Highlights:** Indoor sculpture and flower garden; Botticelli, *Madonna of the Eucharist;* Crivelli, *Saint George and the Dragon;* Giotto, *Presentation of the Child Jesus at the Temple;* Rembrandt, *Self-Portrait;* Sargent, *Isabella Stewart Gardner;* Titian, *The Rape of Europa;* Vermeer, *The Concert.* **Architecture:** 1899–1902 Venetian-style building, created from 15th- and 16th-century fragments, by Sears.

Admission
Donation suggested: Adults $5; seniors & students $2.50; members & children under 12 free. Wed., free. Handicapped accessible.

Hours
Tues., noon–6:30 (July–Aug., noon–5); Wed.–Sun., noon–5. Closed Mon. & holidays.

Tours
For information call (617) 566-1401.

Food & Drink
The Café: Open during museum hours.

Courtyard at the Isabella Stewart Gardner Museum.

Museum of Fine Arts, Boston

465 Huntington Ave., Boston, Mass. 02115
(617) 267-9300

1990 Exhibitions
Thru Feb. 18
Faces of Asia: Portraits from the Permanent Collection
Works from East and South Asia and the Middle East, ranging from Indian paintings and Japanese screens to Chinese hanging and hand scrolls. Catalogue.

Thru Feb. 25
Paintings by Agnes Martin and Sculptures by Donald Judd
Large, light-filled canvases and colorful, geometric sculptures by two artists of the minimalist movement of the 1960s.

Thru Feb. 25
Photographs by Bernhard and Anna Blume
Cologne-based artists present large sequences of staged photographs of panoramic drama.

Boston, Mass.

Thru Mar. 4
Weston's Westons: Portraits and Nudes
Displays 118 figurative works from the master American photographer's collection; includes portraits of James Cagney and e.e. cummings and famous nude studies.

Thru Mar. 11
New American Furniture
Provides a historical perspective of the artisan's interest in technique and material as well as contemporary furniture makers' emphasis on conception and design. Catalogue.

Feb. 7–Apr. 29
Monet in the Nineties: The Series Paintings
Features the artist's famous series of haystacks, poplars, and views of Rouen Cathedral, observed under different light and weather conditions. Catalogue.

Mar. 3–May 9
Shaker Spirit Drawings
Celebrates the 200th anniversary of Hancock Shaker Village in Pittsfield, Mass., with 27 rare drawings of Shaker furniture and crafts.

Mar. 17–July 8
Martin Puryear
Juxtaposes a series of Puryear's sculptures inspired by falcons; exhibited with works from Egyptian, Asiatic, and print collections.

Apr. 11–June 24
†Imperial Taste: Chinese Ceramics from the Percival David Foundation
Includes 56 stunning ceramics collected by Chinese emperors of the Ming, Qing, Song, and Yuan dynasties from the Percival David collection of 1,400 ceramic works.

May 19–July 22
Visual Poetry: The Drawings of Joseph Stella
Sixty works on paper offer insights into the romantic, symbolist, and mystical aspects of Stella's creative expression. Catalogue.

May 25–July 29
†Pierre Bonnard: The Graphic Works
Celebrates the artist's vision of everyday life; includes prints, drawings, illustrated books, oil paintings. Catalogue.

Permanent Collection
Extensive holdings include Egyptian and classical works; Asian and Islamic art including Chinese export porcelain; Peruvian and Coptic textiles and costumes; French and Flemish tapestries; European and American paintings and decorative arts; ship models; ancient musical instruments.
Highlights: Bust of Prince Ankh-haf; Minoan Snake Goddess; Greek Head of Aphrodite; Cassatt, *Five O'clock Tea;* Chen Rong, *Nine Dragon Scroll;* Copley, *Mrs. Samuel*

Quincy; Duccio, *Crucifixion;* Monet, Haystack series; O'Keeffe, *White Rose with Larkspur No. 2;* Picasso, *Rape of the Sabine Women;* Renoir, *Le Bal à Bougival;* Revere, Liberty Bowl; Sargent, *The Daughters of Edward D. Bois;* Turner, *The Slave Ship;* Velázquez, *Don Balthasar Carlos and His Dwarf;* Warhol, *Red Disaster.* **Architecture:** 1909 building by Lowell; 1915 Evans Wing; 1928 White Wing by Stubbins; 1981 West Wing by Pei.

Admission
Adults $6 ($5 when only West Wing is open); seniors $5; children under 16 free. Sat., 10–noon, free. Handicapped accessible.

Hours
Tues., 10–5; Wed., 10–10; Thurs.–Sun., 10–5. West Wing only: Thurs.–Fri., 5–10. Closed Mon. & holidays.

Tours
For information call (617) 267-9300.

Food & Drink
Cafeteria: Tues. & Sat.–Sun., 10–4; Wed.–Fri., 10–8. Fine Arts Restaurant: Tues. & Sat.–Sun., 11:30–2:30; Wed.–Fri., 11:30–2:30 & 5:30–8:30. Galleria Café: Tues. & Sat.–Sun., 10–4; Wed.–Fri., 10–9:30.

The Brooklyn Museum

200 Eastern Pkwy., Brooklyn, N.Y. 11238
(718) 638-5000

1990 Exhibitions
Thru Jan. 8
Lacquer: A Panorama of Asian Decorative Arts
A wide variety of 15th- to 20th-century lacquer objects from Burma, China, Japan, Korea, Iran, and Thailand illustrating regional variations in design, form, and manufacture.

Thru Jan. 22
Curator's Choice: Hispanic Arts of New Mexico
Explores the interaction between Hispanic and Native American artistic traditions; emphasizes 19th-century developments, including polychrome wood sculptures, religious paintings, textiles.

Thru Feb. 19
A Selection from Tissot's "Life of Christ": Watercolors from the Brooklyn Museum
Gouache illustrations executed by the French artist between 1886 and 1894.

Reception Dress, c. 1903, by Jacques Doucet. From *The Opulent Era: Fashions of Worth, Pingat, and Doucet* at The Brooklyn Museum, thru Feb. 26.

Brooklyn, N.Y.

Thru Feb. 26
The Opulent Era: Fashions of Worth, Doucet, and Pingat
Features 75 costumes, 1885–1905, in the first major exhibition to compare the dominant house of Worth and lesser-known ateliers. Catalogue.

Thru Mar. 5
David Mach: Grand Lobby Installation
A site-specific installation incorporating thousands of cast-off articles such as books, magazines, and shoes to represent the excesses of commodity culture.

Thru Mar. 26
Image and Reflection: Adolph Gottlieb's Pictographs and African Sculpture
Features African, Oceanic, and Pre-Columbian objects supplemented by paintings by Gottlieb.

Feb. 9–June 18
American Artists of the Alfred Stieglitz Circle: Works from the Brooklyn Museum
Paintings and works on paper by artists associated with the noted photographer and his gallery, "291"; includes works by Dove, Marin, O'Keeffe, Stieglitz, Walkowitz, Weber.

Feb. 9–Aug. 6
Chinese Cloisonné and Highlights from the Permanent Chinese Collection
Displays 34 cloisonné vessels of exceptional craftsmanship from the Ming dynasty through the Quianlong era.

Mar. 2–May 7
†Czech Modernism: 1900–1945
Presents the evolution of the Czech avant-garde from expressionism through surrealism; focuses on the interdisciplinary aspects of painting, sculpture, works on paper, photography, film. Catalogue.

Mar. 16–June 4
Komar & Melamid
Two interrelated multipanel mixedmedia works by Russian-born contemporary artists who incorporate sequences of images related to personal and collective memory.

April 20–June 25
Facing History: The Image of the Black in American Art
Examines how social and cultural attitudes and historic events affected artists' representations of black society, 1750–1930; includes work by Benton, Copley, Eakins, Homer, Johnson, Mount, Sargent, Wood.

May 18–July 30
†The Intimate Interiors of Edouard Vuillard
Paintings from the 1890s by the postimpressionist master who was a founder of the Nabis, an offshoot of the symbolist movement. Catalogue.

Brooklyn, N.Y.

May 18–Oct. 29
In Pursuit of the Spiritual: Oceanic Art given by Mr. and Mrs. John A. Friede and Mrs. Melville W. Hall
A selection of artifacts including headdresses, musical instruments, and sculptures.

May 25–July 16
Recent Drawing Acquisitions
Includes works by Barry, Bellmer, Buren, Hartley, Klimt, LeWitt, Miró, and Steir.

June 15–Sept. 3
Winnifred Outz
A three-dimensional site-specific installation for the museum's grand lobby by the contemporary American artist.

July 27–Sept. 24
"By Accident of Place" : Photographs by W. Eugene Smith
Images by American photo-journalists, 1918–1978.

Sept. 7–Nov. 1
Festival Arts of the Caribbean

Sept. 21–Dec. 3
Joseph Kosuth
A site-specific installation for the museum's Grand Lobby by a leading proponent of conceptual art.

Sept. 21–Jan. 7, 1991
Albert Pinkham Ryder
Includes 78 paintings of intimate landscapes and pastoral themes, rare decorative objects on gilded leather and mahogany panels, Near Eastern subjects, early marine paintings. Catalogue.

Permanent Collection
Ancient Egyptian, Greek, and Roman art; ancient Middle Eastern and Islamic art; Asian, Pre-Columbian, African, Oceanic art; American and European paintings and sculptures; decorative arts; costumes and textiles; prints and drawings; American period rooms; contemporary art.
Highlights: Assyrian reliefs; Rodin Sculpture Gallery; sculpture garden; Eakins, *William Rush Carving the Allegorical Figure of the Schuylkill.* **Architecture:** 1893 neoclassical building by McKim, Mead, and White; completion of museum by Arata Isozaki and Associates and James Stewart Polshek and Partners.

Admission
Donation suggested: Adults $3; seniors $1; students with ID $1.50; children under 12 accompanied by adult free. Handicapped accessible.

Hours
Mon. & Wed.–Sun., 10–5. Closed Tues., Jan. 1, Thanksgiving, Dec. 25.

Buffalo, N.Y.

Tours
Call (718) 638-5000, ext. 221.

Food & Drink
Museum Café: Mon. & Wed.–Sun., 10–4.

Albright-Knox Art Gallery

1285 Elmwood Ave., Buffalo, N.Y. 14222
(716) 882-8700

Reclining Figure No. 4, 1961, by Henry Moore. Albright-Knox Art Gallery.

1990 Exhibitions
Thru Jan. 7
10 + 10: Contemporary Soviet and American Painters
Works representing the new avant-garde in the Soviet Union and America.

Jan. 20–Mar. 11
Hamish Fulton: Selected Walks 1969–1989
Presents photo and text works by the British artist known for his "walks" through the Americas. Examines the Yucatán, southwest United States, and Canadian tundra and includes works representing his interest in indigenous people.

May 12–July 1
Imagenes Liricas/New Spanish Visions
Features the works of eight Spanish artists from the post-Franco era.

July 14–Sept. 2
Frank Lloyd Wright: Preserving an Architectural Heritage, Decorative Designs from the Domino's Pizza Collection

Sept. 16–Nov. 4
Morgan Russell: A Retrospective
The first major retrospective of the pioneering American modernist; includes his well-known work *Synchromy in Orange: To Form, 1913–14* from the permanent collection.

Nov. 17–Jan. 6, 1991
John Pfahl
Retrospective comprises provocative images of contemporary landscapes by an internationally known color photographer.

Permanent Collection
Sculpture from 3000 B.C. to the present; 18th-century English and 19th-century French and American painting; noted holdings of modern art. **Highlights:** Gauguin, *Spirit of the Dead Watching* and *Yellow Christ;* Hogarth, *The Lady's Last Stake;* Kiefer, *The Milky Way;* Lichtenstein, *Picture and Pitcher;* Matisse, *La Musique;* Moore, *Reclining Figure;* Pollock, *Convergence;* Samaras, *Mirrored Room;*

Cambridge, Mass.

Segal, *Cinema*. **Architecture:** 1905 Greek-revival building by Green; 1962 addition with sculpture court by Bunshaft of Skidmore, Owings, and Merrill.

Admission
Donation suggested. Handicapped accessible.

Hours
Tues.–Sat., 11–5; Sun., noon–5. Closed Mon., Jan. 1, Thanksgiving, Dec. 25.

Tours
Wed.–Thurs. at 12:15; Sat.–Sun. at 1:30. For reservations, call (716) 882-8700, ext. 226.

Food & Drink
Garden Restaurant: Tues.–Sat., 11–3:45; Sun., noon–3.

The Harvard Art Museums

The Arthur M. Sackler Museum
485 Broadway, Cambridge, Mass. 02138
(617) 495-9400

1990 Exhibitions
Thru Jan. 28
Rembrandt and His School: Drawings from the Museum Boymans-van Beuningen, Rotterdam
Sixty-five works, including 15 drawings by Rembrandt, display the exceptional range of 17th-century Dutch draftsmanship. Catalogue.

Feb. 24–Apr. 8
From Fontainebleau to the Louvre: French Master Drawings from the Seventeenth Century
Works by such leading French artists as Poussin and Vouet document the birth and triumph of French classicism.

May 26–July 22
The Fredric Wertham Collection
Contemporary works bequeathed to Busch-Reisinger; includes paintings by Zelda Fitzgerald, Lissitzky, Schwitters.

Permanent Collection
Renowned collections of ancient Chinese art, Japanese prints, Indian and Islamic paintings, Greek and classical sculpture, Roman coins; Oriental carpets. **Highlights:** Chinese jades, cave reliefs, bronzes; Japanese woodblock prints; Persian paintings and examples of calligraphy.
Architecture: 1985 building by Stirling.

Tours
Tues.–Fri. at 2. Call (617) 495-4544.

Cambridge, Mass.

Busch-Reisinger Museum
29 Kirkland St., Cambridge, Mass. 02138
(617) 495-9400

Permanent Collection
Selections from the permanent collection are on display at the Fogg Art Museum during 1990. Specializes in art of German-speaking Europe: 16th-century painting; late medieval, Renaissance, and baroque sculpture; 18th-century porcelain from Germany, Austria, the Low Countries; 20th-century art. **Architecture:** 1921 building by Bestelmeyer; 1990 building by Gwathmey, Siegel, and Associates under construction.

After the Bath, 1890–92, by Edgar Degas. Fogg Art Museum.

Fogg Art Museum
32 Quincy St., Cambridge, Mass. 02138
(617) 495-9400

1990 Exhibitions
Thru Jan. 14
Understanding Nature: American Zoological Art from the Museum of Comparative Zoology
More than thirty 19th- and 20th-century paintings, watercolors, drawings, and notebooks by Audubon, Benson, La Farge, Wilson, and others.

Jan. 20–Mar. 18
Envisioning America: Prints, Drawings, and Photographs by George Grosz and His Contemporaries
Studies how American myths of the Wild West and the city influenced the art of the 1920s in Germany.

Permanent Collection
Masterpieces of Western painting, sculpture, graphic art. The Fogg will house the Busch-Reisinger collection during 1990. **Highlights:** Drawings by Michelangelo and Rembrandt; Fra Angelico, *Crucifixion;* van Gogh, *Self-Portrait;* Ingres, *Odalisque;* Monet, *Gare Saint-Lazare;* Picasso, *Mother and Child;* Poussin, *Infant Bacchus Entrusted to the Nymphs;* Renoir, *Seated Bather.* **Architecture:** 1927 Neo-Georgian exterior; Italianate courtyard.

Tours
Tues.–Fri. at 11. Call (617) 495-4544.

All Three Museums:

Admission
Adults $4; seniors & students $2.50; age 18 & under free; Sat., 10–noon, free. Handicapped accessible.

Hours
Tues.–Sun., 10–5. Closed Mon., Jan. 1, July 4, Thanksgiving, Dec. 24–25.

Chadds Ford, Pa.

Brandywine River Museum

Brandywine Conservancy, Chadds Ford, Pa. 19317
(215) 388-7601; 459-1900

1990 Exhibitions
Thru Jan. 7
A Brandywine Christmas
Decorated trees, model trains, children's illustrations, and selections from an automotive art and toy collection.

Jan. 13–Mar. 11
Highlights from the Permanent Collection

Mar. 18–May 21
Artists in Line: An Al Hirshfeld Retrospective
Spans the career of the important American illustrator.

Permanent Collection
American art with special emphasis on the art of the Brandywine region. Nineteenth- and 20th-century landscapes by Cropsey, Doughty, Lathrop, Moran, Richards, Sword, Tatnell; still-life paintings, including 19th-century trompe l'oeil works by Carlson, Cope, Evans, Haberle, Harnett, Peale, Peto, Ream; illustrations by Darley and the noted Brandywine Valley artist Howard Pyle. **Highlights:** Paintings by three generations of Wyeths. **Architecture:** 1864 Hoffman's Mill by Grieves.

Admission
Adults $4; seniors $2.50; students with ID $2; children, 6–12, $1.50; members & children under 6 free. Handicapped accessible.

Hours
Daily, 9:30–4:30; Dec. 26–30, 9:30–8. Closed Dec. 25.

Tours
Available Mon.–Fri., 9:30–2:30, by reservation. Call (215) 459-1900, ext. 166.

Food & Drink
Restaurant: 11–3.

The Mint Museum of Art

2730 Randolph Rd., Charlotte, N.C. 28207
(704) 337-2000; 333-MINT (recorded)

1990 Exhibitions
Thru Feb. 11
A Celebration of Photography
Investigates the diversity of the medium in honor of the 150th anniversary of photography.

Charlotte, N.C.

My Friend Brien, 1913, by Robert Henri. The Mint Museum of Art.

Thru Mar. 4
Contemporary Icons and Explorations: The Goldstrom Family Collection
Catalogue.

Apr. 1–May 27
Zenga: Brushstrokes of Enlightenment
Over 70 pieces from the Japanese Edo period (1615–1887) illustrate the aesthetics and technical mastery of Zen painters. Catalogue.

Aug. 19–Oct. 7
Art That Works: The Decorative Arts of the Eighties, Crafted in America
One hundred works by foremost designer craftsmen. Book.

Oct. 26–Jan. 6, 1991
That's All Folks! Bugs Bunny and Friends
A comprehensive overview of the Warner Bros. animation studio, which has produced the cartoon characters that have become part of American folklore.

Permanent Collection
Pre-Columbian and African art; European painting; American works by Cole, Inness, Prendergast, Stuart; regional crafts; American pottery; historic artifacts of North Carolina's Piedmont region; gold coins. **Highlights:** Dalton collection of works by Constable, Eakins, Homer, Remington, Wyeth; Delhom Gallery of pottery and porcelain from ancient times to the 18th century; Ghirlandaijo, *Madonna and Child with Four Saints;* West, *Agriculture Aided by Arts and Commerce.* **Architecture:** 1835 Federal-style building by Strickland; 1967 Delhom Gallery by Odell and Associates; 1985 Dalton Wing by Clark, Tibble, Harris, and Li.

Admission
Adults $2; children, 4–12, $1; members free. Tues., 5–10 & second Sunday of each month, free. Handicapped accessible.

Hours
Tues., 10–10; Wed.–Sat., 10–5; Sun. & Thanksgiving Day, 1–6. Closed Mon., Jan. 1, Dec. 25.

Tours
Daily at 2., or call (704) 337-2000 for reservations.

Other Collections of Note

**Hunter Museum of Art
10 Bluff View, Chattanooga, Tenn. 37403
(615) 267-0968**

Chicago, Ill.

The Art Institute of Chicago

**Michigan Ave. at Adams St., Chicago, Ill. 60603
(312) 443-3600; 443-3500 (recorded)**

1990 Exhibitions
Indefinite
Ellsworth Kelly
An installation of six paintings.

Thru Jan. 2
American Art since World War II: Recent Acquisitions
Features works by Fischl, Guston, Johns, de Kooning, Marden, Nauman, Neel, Rothenberg, Ruscha, Smith, Smithson, Twombly, Warhol, Wesselman.

Thru Jan. 22
European Textile Masterpieces from Coptic Times through the Nineteenth Century
Features embroidered, printed, and woven textiles as well as lace from the permanent collection.

Feb. 10–Apr. 1
Yoruba: Nine Centuries of African Art and Thought
Explores the dynamic history and contemporary vitality of the Yoruba people of Nigeria; features about 100 objects in various media, including 17 significant works from museums in Ife and Lagos.

Feb. 28–June 25
Designed by the Yard–Twentieth-Century Pattern Repeats
Presents the work of internationally renowned textile designers and architects.

Mar. 10–June 3
What's New: Mexico City
Contemporary Latin photography from Mexico City.

May 1–July 1
Emilio Ambasz: Architecture, Exhibition, Industrial, and Graphic Design
A comprehensive retrospective by one of this century's most influential architects and designers.

May 12–July 29
The Gerald S. Elliott Collection
Surveys contemporary art since the mid-1960s; includes works by André, Clemente, Jenney, Judd, Kiefer, Mangold, Marden, Shapiro, Schnabel. Catalogue.

May 19–Aug. 12
Monet in the Nineties: The Series Paintings
Features the artist's famous series of haystacks, poplars, and views of Rouen Cathedral, observed under different light and weather conditions. Catalogue.

Chicago, Ill.

July 26–Oct. 28
Lenore Tawney Retrospective
Includes fiber works, boxes, drawings, postcard collages, and sculptures by the contemporary American artist.

Sept. 1–Nov. 11
Ed Paschke: Paintings
Works including figurative compositions and video images span the artist's career from 1968 to 1988. Catalogue.

Sept. 8–Nov. 25
From Poussin to Matisse: The Russian Taste for French Paintings, A Loan from the USSR
An exchange exhibition with the USSR's Hermitage and Pushkin museums; includes works by Bonnard, Boucher, Cézanne, Gauguin, Lorrain, Matisse, Poussin, Renoir.

Sept. 15–Dec. 2
The New Vision: Photography between the World Wars
Celebrates the 150th anniversary of photography with 115 vintage images illustrating the photographic revolution in 20th-century vision in Europe and America. Includes works by Abbott, Bayer, Brancusi, Bourke-White, Cartier-Bresson, Evans, Magritte, Man Ray, Rodchenko, Stieglitz, Weston. Catalogue.

Permanent Collection
Spans forty centuries of art: Chinese bronzes, ceramics, jades; Japanese prints; Greek and Roman sculptures, glass, jewelry, mosaics; works from Africa and Oceania; ancient Mesoamerican and Peruvian ceramics and figurative art; Harding collection of arms and armor; acclaimed impressionist collection. **Highlights:** Caillebotte, *Paris: A Rainy Day;* Cassatt, *The Bath;* Goya, *The Capture of Maragato by Fray Pedro;* El Greco, *Assumption of the Virgin;* Monet, *The River;* a large group of Picassos; Seurat, *Sunday Afternoon on the Island of La Grand Jatte;* Wood, *American Gothic;* six extraordinary panels from a large, early Renaissance altarpiece by Giovanni di Paolo depicting the life of Saint John the Baptist; reconstructed Chicago Stock Exchange Trading Room designed by Adler and Sullivan. **Architecture:** 1894 beaux-arts building by Shepley, Rutan, and Coolidge; 1986 renovation by Skidmore, Owings, and Merrill; 1988 South Building by Hammond, Beeby, and Babka.

Admission
Suggested donation: Adults $5; seniors, students with ID, children $2.50. Tues., free. Handicapped accessible.

Hours
Mon. & Wed.–Fri., 10:30–4:30; Tues., 10:30–8; Sat., 10–5; Sun. & holidays, noon–5. Closed Dec. 25.

Tours
Call (312) 443-3530.

Chicago, Ill.

Food & Drink
Cafeteria: Mon. & Wed.–Sat., 10:30–4; Tues., 10:30–7; Sun., noon–4. Dining Room and La Promenade Café: Mon.–Sat., 11–2:30. Garden Restaurant: Summer, Mon.–Sat., 11–3; Sun., noon–3; Tues., 4–7.

Museum of Contemporary Art

237 East Ontario St., Chicago, Ill. 60611
(312) 280-2660; 280-5161 (recorded)

1990 Exhibitions
Thru Jan. 28
The Photography of Invention: American Pictures of the 1980s
Celebrates photography's 150th anniversary with 160 works by 80 American photographers. Catalogue.

Thru Feb. 4
Options 37
Artist to be announced.

Feb. 17–Apr. 15
Options 38: Richard Rezac

Feb. 17–Apr. 22
Robert Longo
Documents the thematic development of the artist's work, from his early performance pieces to his current monumental reliefs and constructions. Catalogue.

May 5–June–17
Options 39
Artist to be announced.

May 5–June 17
Georg Baselitz

Permanent Collection
Twentieth-century paintings, drawings, sculptures, prints, photographs, films, videotapes, audio pieces by such artists as Bacon, Braque, Calder, Christo, Dubuffet, Duchamp, Magritte, Oldenburg, Paschke, Rauschenberg, Segal.
Highlights: Bacon, *Man in Blue Box;* new acquisitions includes works by Bevys, Boxqeisal, Jackson; Simonds' *Dwellings.* **Architecture:** Former bakery renovated 1969; 1979 addition by Booth; 1991 addition by Booth planned.

Admission
Adults $4; seniors, students, children under 16 $2; Tues., free. Handicapped accessible.

Chicago, Ill.

Hours
Tues.–Sat., 10–5; Sun., noon–5. Closed Mon., Jan. 1, Thanksgiving, Dec. 25. Galleries may be closed for installation between exhibitions.

Tours
Tues.–Fri. at 12:15; Sat.–Sun. at 1 & 3. For group tour reservations call (312) 280-2697.

Food & Drink
Site Café Bookstore: Tues.–Sat., 11–5; Sun., noon–5.

Terra Museum of American Art

**666 North Michigan Ave., Chicago, Ill. 60611
(312) 664-3939**

1990 Exhibitions
Thru Jan. 7
Frontier America: Art and Treasures of the Old West from the Buffalo Bill Historical Center

Jan. 23–Mar. 11
Abstract Expressionism: Other Dimensions
Features small-scale paintings from the New York school.

Mar. 17–Apr. 29
American Paintings from a Century of Collecting: The Maier Museum of Art, Randolph-Macon Woman's College Collection
The evolution of American art through the early 19th century is illustrated in 50 works by Chase, Cole, Davies, Dove, Durand, Kensett, Marin, O'Keeffe, Robinson, and Twachtman. Catalogue.

May 5–July 8
Early American Photography: The First Fifty Years
A comprehensive showing of works by the 19th-century pioneers of American photography. Catalogue.

July 14–Sept. 9
Morgan Russell: A Retrospective
The first major retrospective of the pioneering American modernist.

Sept. 15–Nov. 11
Winslow Homer: The Gloucester Watercolors, 1873

Nov. 17–Jan. 13, 1991
Winslow Homer in the 1890s: Prout's Neck Observed
Works from the Memorial Art Gallery of the University of Rochester.

Permanent Collection
Based on the personal collection of Daniel Terra, spanning two centuries of American art. **Highlights:** Bingham, *The Jolly Flatboatmen;* Morse, *Gallery of the Louvre;* works by Cassatt, Homer, Sargent, Whistler. **Architecture:** 1987 building by Booth and Hansen.

Admission
Adults $4; seniors $2.50; students $1; children under 11 free. Handicapped accessible.

Hours
Tues., noon–8; Wed.–Sat., 10–5; Sun., noon–5. Closed Mon. & holidays.

Tours
Daily at noon & 2. For school and group tour reservations call (312) 664-3939.

Cincinnati Art Museum

Eden Park, Cincinnati, Ohio 45202
(513) 721-5204

1990 Exhibitions
Thru Jan. 7
The Alice and Harris Weston Collection of Postwar Art
Features internationally renowned artists, including Albers, de Kooning, Rauschenberg, Warhol. Catalogue.

Thru Mar. 4
The Steckelmann Collection: One Hundred Years of African Art at the Cincinnati Art Museum
Celebrates the establishment of the collection made possible by a fund subscribed to by Prominent Cincinnatians in 1890.

Jan. 19–May 20
Innovation and Tradition: Twentieth-Century Japanese Prints from the Howard and Caroline Porter Collection
Focuses on the extraordinary vitality and innovative genius of modern Japanese printmaking. Catalogue.

Feb. 7–Apr. 8
Carthage: A Mosaic of Ancient Tunisia
Includes bronzes, statues, jewelry, pottery, and coins from about 800 B.C. to A.D. 700.

Mar. 16–May 27
French and American Studio Ceramics
Displays works produced in the 1930s by eight studio potters.

Two Children, c. 1820, American, artist unknown. From *The Art of Folk Art,* at the Cincinnati Art Museum May 11–Sept. 2.

Cincinnati, Ohio

May 11–Sept. 2
The Fine Art of Folk Art
Features quilts, weather vanes, scrimshaw, furniture, sculpture, and works on paper from the 18th to 20th centuries. Catalogue.

May 19–July 1
Summoning of the Souls: Treasures from the Tombs of China
Explores life in Han dynasty China (12th–2d century B.C.) through silks, lacquerware, and wooden tomb figurines excavated at the tomb of the marquis of Dai at Mawangdui in Hunan province. Catalogue.

June 9–Sept. 30
The Shadow of the Mainsail
Displays prints of maritime themes from the 16th to 20th centuries by Dürer, Feininger, Whistler, and others.

June 15–Sept. 30
Fakes and Forgeries: The Deceiver's Art
Presents works once thought to be by such artists as Hals, Millet, and Rodin, now proven to be fakes.

Permanent Collection
Features significant Greek, Roman, Etruscan holdings; Near and Far Eastern art; art from Africa, Pre-Columbian America, the South Pacific; North American Indian art; French, Spanish, Italian medieval sculpture; decorative arts; ancient musical instruments; American paintings by Cassatt, Church, Cole, Copley, Sargent; 20th-century art; work by Cincinnati artists. **Highlights:** Excellent Near Eastern collection (both ancient and Islamic); Corot, *Mantes;* Gainsborough, *Portrait of Mrs. Philip Thicknesse;* Sargent, *Italian Girl with Fan;* Titian, *Philip II of Spain;* Wood, *Daughters of the Revolution.*

Admission
Adults $3; college students $2; seniors $1.50; members & age 17 & under free. Sat., free. Entrance fee for selected exhibitions. Handicapped accessible.

Hours
Tues. & Thurs.–Sat., 10–5, Wed., 10–9; Sun., 1–5. Closed Mon. & holidays.

Tours
Wed. & Sat.–Sun. at 2.

Food & Drink
Terrace Court Restaurant: Tues.–Sat., 11:30–2:30.

The Cleveland Museum of Art

11150 East Blvd., Cleveland, Ohio 44106
(216) 421-7340

1990 Exhibitions
Thru Jan. 28
Cervin Robinson: Cleveland, Ohio
One hundred gelatin silver prints taken of the city commissioned by the museum.

Thru Jan. 28
From Fontainebleau to the Louvre: French Master Drawings from the Seventeenth Century
Works by such leading French artists as Poussin and Vouet document the birth and triumph of French classicism.

Feb. 28–Apr. 15
Bourke-White: A Retrospective
Features 120 works appearing in magazines *Life* and *Fortune* by the master photographer.

Apr. 4–May 27
May Show for 1990
The 71st annual juried exhibition of works by artists from Ohio's Western Reserve region.

July 27–Aug. 19
Photography until Now
Celebrates the sesquicentennial of Daguerre's first photographic achievements; includes about 250 photographs dating from the 1830s to the present.

Sept. 19–Nov. 18
Winslow Homer and American Realism
Draws together paintings by Bellows, George, Homer, Hopper, and Kent to examine the ways Homer assimilated contemporary artistic developments and helped shape them.

Oct. 10–Dec. 9
Yoruba: Nine Centuries of African Art and Thought
Explores the dynamic history and contemporary vitality of the Yoruba people of Nigeria; features about 100 objects in various media, including 17 significant works from museums in Ife and Lagos.

Nov. 13–Jan. 13, 1991
Five Centuries of Old Master Drawings from the Museum Boymans-van Beuningen, Rotterdam
Features the finest 15th- to 19th-century drawings from the museum's renowned collection; includes drawings by Bruegel, Delacroix, Dürer, van Eyck, Fragonard, Goya, Ingres, Rembrandt, Rubens, Tintoretto, Van Dyck.

South African Miners, c. 1950, by Margaret Bourke-White. From *Bourke-White: A Retrospective* at The Cleveland Museum of Art, Feb. 28–Apr. 15.

Cody, Wyo.

Permanent Collection
Comprehensive holdings of art from antiquity to the present. Important Asian and medieval Western collections; late 19th- and 20th-century art; coins; textiles; photographs; prints; drawings. **Highlights:** Chinese paintings from the Song and Ming dynasties; Warring States Period *Cranes and Serpents;* Cambodian Krishna Govardhana; the Gwelph Treasure, 18th-century French decorative art; sculpture garden; Caravaggio, *Crucifixion of Saint Andrew;* Kline, *Accent Grave;* Monet, *Water Lilies;* Picasso, *La Vie;* Rubens, *Portrait of his Wife, Isabella Brant;* Ryder, *Death on a Pale Horse;* Turner, *Burning of the Houses of Parliament;* Zurbarán, *Holy House of Nazareth.* **Architecture:** 1916 Neo-Georgian building by Hubbell and Benes; 1971 addition by Smith and Breuer.

Admission
Free. Handicapped accessible.

Hours
Tues. & Thurs.–Fri., 10–5:45; Wed., 10–9:45; Sat., 9–4:45; Sun., 1–5:45. Closed Mon., Jan. 1, July 4, Thanksgiving, Dec. 25.

Tours
Daily at 1:30.

Food & Drink
Museum Café: Tues.–Fri., noon–4:30; Sat., 11:45–4:15; Sun., 1–4:45. $2 min. Tues.–Sat., noon–2.

Buffalo Bill Historical Center

P.O. Box 1000
720 Sheridan Ave., Cody, Wyo. 82414
(307) 587-4771

1990 Exhibitions
Mar. 1–Apr. 20
Wyoming by the Book: Territorial Imprints, 1866–1890
Presents the most important works printed in Wyoming before statehood; shows how the emergence of a literate culture in Wyoming helped assure ultimate statehood. Catalogue.

Apr. 24–July 15
Rendezvous to Roundup: The First One Hundred Years of Art in Wyoming
Features 60 works of art, beginning in 1837 with the first Wyoming artist trained in Europe, Alfred Jacob Miller. Catalogue.

July 25–Nov. 30 (Plains Indian Museum)
Wounded Knee Anniversary

Mar. 1–July 1
1869–1890 Territorial Imprints–McDonald Collection

Permanent Collection
Four museums in one: **Buffalo Bill Museum** contains personal and historical memorabilia of William F. "Buffalo Bill" Cody; **Plains Indian Museum** displays materials reflecting the artistic expressions of the Arapaho, Blackfeet, Cheyenne, Crow, Shoshone, Sioux, Gros Ventre tribes; **Whitney Gallery of Western Art** documents the beauty of the American West through paintings and sculptures by American artists Bierstadt, Catlin, Miller, Moran, Remington, Russell, Sharp, Wyeth; **Winchester Arms Museum** presents the story of the development of firearms in America through its comprehensive collection.

Admission
Adults $5; seniors $4.25; students $3.25; children $2; families $14; children under 6 free. Group rates by request. Handicapped accessible.

Hours
May & Sept., daily, 8–8; June–Aug., daily, 7–10; Oct., daily, 8–5; Mar. & Nov., Tues.–Sun., 10–3; Apr., Tues.–Sun., 8–5. Closed Dec.–Feb. & holidays.

Tours
Call (307) 587-4771 for information.

Food & Drink
Restaurant: May–Sept., 9–3.

Columbus Museum of Art

**480 East Broad St., Columbus, Ohio 43215
(614) 221-6801**

1990 Exhibitions
Thru Jan. 7
A Salute to Daguerre
Features French daguerreotypes from the George Eastman House and early American daguerreotypes from Ohio State University's Rinhart Collection.

Thru Feb. 4
The Art of Paul Manship
Reevaluates the accomplishments of the renowned art deco artist; includes sculptures, medals, works on paper. Book.

Thru Feb. 4
Linear Grace: Evening Couture of the 1920s and 1930s
Women's evening couture from the Historic Costume and Textiles Collections of Ohio State University.

Columbus, Ohio

Feb. 18–Apr. 15
Wild Spirits, Strong Medicine: African Art and the Wilderness
Examines the dichotomy between nature and African culture; includes masks, headdresses, sculptures, costumes, and hunter's charms from various African cultures. Catalogue.

May 6–June 10
Will Hawkins and Aminah Brenda Robinson
Features paintings by the contemporary artists.

Sept. 16–Nov. 25
Contemporary Soviet Painting
Examines the link between the early and new Russian avant-garde and analyzes the impact of changing Communist ideology on Russian art of the past 25 years. Catalogue.

Permanent Collection
Pre-Columbian and South Pacific art; Oriental ceramics; 16th- and 17th-century Dutch and Flemish painting; 18th- to 20th-century European and American painting; decorative art. Galleries are arranged thematically, each focusing on works of similar subject matter, period, or culture. **Highlights:** Bellows paintings and lithographs; Boucher, *Earth;* Degas, *Dancer at Rest;* Ingres, *Raphael and the Fornarina;* O'Keeffe, *Autumn Leaves;* Rubens, *Christ Triumphant over Sin and Death;* sculpture garden with works by Archipenko, Maillol, Manzù, Moore. **Architecture:** 1931 Italianate building; 1974 addition.

Admission
Adults $3.50; seniors, students with ID, children, 6–17, $1. Fri., free. Handicapped accessible.

Hours
Tues.–Fri. & Sun., 11–5; Wed., 11–9; Sat., 10–5. Closed Mon., Jan. 1, July 4, Thanksgiving, Dec. 25.

Tours
Fri. at noon. For group tour reservations call (614) 221-6801 6–8 weeks in advance.

Food & Drink
The Palette: Tues.–Fri., 11:30–1:30; Sat. & Sun., noon–2.

Earth: Vertumnus and Pomona, 1749, by Francois Boucher. Columbus Museum of Art

Dallas Museum of Art

1717 North Harwood, Dallas, Tex. 75201
(214) 922-1200

1990 Exhibitions
Thru Feb. 25
Black Art–Ancestral Legacy
Explores African cultural roots in black visual arts in the U.S. and the Caribbean during the last 50 years. Catalogue.

Apr. 8–June 10
†*Gold of Africa: Jewelry and Ornaments from Ghana, Côte D'Ivoire, Mali, and Senegal*
Jewelry and royal regalia primarily made by the Akan-speaking peoples in the 19th and 20th centuries. Catalogue.

Apr. 8–June 10
Gold of Greece, Jewelry and Ornaments from the Benaki Collection; Gold of the Ancient Americas
Accompanies *Gold of Africa* exhibition.

May 13–July 15
Ed Paschke: Paintings
Works including figurative compsitions and video images span the artist's career from 1968 to 1988. Catalogue.

July 8–Sept. 2
Treasures of American Folk Art from the Abby Aldrich Rockefeller Folk Art Center
Features 18th to 19th-century folk art objects, including paintings, fraktur, trade and shop signs, weather vanes, toys, decoys, quilts, coverlets. Catalogue.

Early Fall
Long-term Loan of Egyptian Works from the Collection of the Museum of Fine Arts, Boston

Permanent Collection
Significant holdings of Pre-Columbian and African art; 18th- to 20th-century European and American paintings; decorative arts, including American furniture and English silver; prints; drawings; photographs. **Highlights:** Peruvian gold; Reves collection of Chinese porcelain; antique furniture; ironwork; impressionist and postimpressionist paintings; drawings; watercolors; Brancusi, *Beginning of the World;* Matisse, *Ivy in Flowers;* Oldenburg, *Stake Hitch;* Kelly, *Untitled* (commissioned for sculpture garden). **Architecture:** 1984 building of Indiana limestone by Edward Larabee Barnes Associates; 1985 recreated Mediterranean villa houses Reves collection.

Admission
Free. Entrance fee for selected exhibitions. Handicapped accessible.

Dayton, Ohio

Hours
Tues–Sat., 10–5; Thurs., 10–9; Sun., noon–5. Closed Mon., Jan. 1, Thanksgiving, Dec. 25.

Food & Drink
Gallery Buffet: Tues.–Sat., 11:30–2; Thurs. dinner, 6–8, by reservation; Sun., noon–2. Bar: Tues.–Sat., 11:30–4:30; Thurs., 11:30–7:30; Sun., noon–4:30.

The Dayton Art Institute

P.O. Box 941, Forest and Riverview Aves., Dayton, Ohio 45405-0941
(513) 223-5277

1990 Exhibitions
Thru Jan. 14
Leaves from the Bodhi Tree: The Art of Pala India
First major national exhibition of 250 objects from the Pala dynasty (8th–12th cent.).

Jan. 16–May 28
Art that Flies
Explores the properties of flight on forced air; includes a display of kites, sculptures, slides, videos.

Feb. 2–Apr. 1
Native American Art and Artifacts from the Permanent Collection

Apr. 28–June 3
That's All Folks! Bugs Bunny and Friends
A comprehensive overview of the Warner Bros. animation studio, which has produced the cartoon characters that have become part of American folklore.

June 30–Aug. 12
Design Revolution: Ceramics from the Weimar Republic
Nearly 100 examples of brightly decorated mass-produced art deco ceramics of the Bauhaus movement, 1919–33.

Permanent Collection
American, European, Asian, Oceanic, African art; Ponderosa collection of contemporary American art. **Highlights:** Greco-Roman Aphrodite Pudica; Hopper, *High Noon;* Monet, *Water Lilies;* Rubens, *Portrait of Daniel Nijs;* Warhol, *Russell Means;* Experiencenter, where visitors experience art by seeing and doing. **Architecture:** 1930 Italianate building by Green; 1981 entry by Levin Porter Smith Inc.

Admission
Adults $2; seniors & students with ID $1; members & children under 18 free. First Sat. each month, free. Handicapped accessible.

Mickey Mouse, 1981, by Andy Warhol. The Dayton Art Institute.

Denver, Colo.

Hours
Tues.–Sun., noon–5. Closed Mon. (except holidays) & Dec. 25.

Tours
Call (513) 223-5277 for information.

Denver Art Museum

**100 West 14th Ave. Pkwy., Denver, Colo. 80204
(303) 575-2793**

1990 Exhibitions
Thru Feb. 4
Chinese Textiles and Costumes
Qing dynasty robes and accessories from the permanent collection.

Thru Feb. 4
Deborah Butterfield Sculpture
Four full-scale horses, including the museum's *Orion*.

Thru Mar. 18
Karl Bodmer Prints
Portraits and landscapes from the Bodmer collection depict life on the upper Missouri River in the 1830s.

Thru May 6
Bill Henson Photography
The Australian artist creates a floor-to-ceiling installation with large color images for his first U.S. solo exhibition.

Thru May 27
Contemporary Chinese Ceramics from Taiwan
Sixty works by noted contemporary artists.

Thru Apr. 1
Frontier America: Art and Treasures of the Old West from the Buffalo Bill Historical Center

Thru June 3
The Gund Collection of Western Art

Feb. 24–May 27
From the Loom
Features 19th-century weavings.

Mar. 3–June 3
Paul Gillis: Paintings and Jim Green: Sound Installation
Includes paintings and works on paper by Denver artist Gillis and a site-specific environment constructed by Green.

Mar. 24–Aug. 26
Santa Fe Style Native American Paintings

Denver, Colo.

Apr. 7–June 3
I Dream a World: Portraits of Black Women Who Changed America
Seventy-five portraits by Pulitzer Prize winning photographer Brian Lanker of Maya Angelou, Shirley Chisholm, Odetta, Rosa Parks, Sarah Vaughn, and others. Catalogue.

Apr. 28–June 24
Colorado 1990
Highlights works by leading Colorado artists.

June 2–Aug. 5
Sandy Skoglund: Red Fox Installation

June 23–Sept. 9
†*Little People of the Earth: Pre-Columbian Burial Ceramics*
Over 150 "pretty lady" and "gingerbread" figures representing a wide geographic area and broad time period (c. 3000 B.C.–A.D. 900).

June 30–Oct. 14
Carley Warren Sculpture
Painted wood constructions by the Denver artist.

July 5–Sept. 9
Childe Hassam: An Island Garden Revisited
First major exhibition to focus solely on the artist's impressionist paintings of the Isles of Shoals. Includes oils, watercolors, pastels. Catalogue.

July 21–Sept. 16
†*Gold of Africa: Jewelry and Ornaments from Ghana, Côte d'Ivoire, Mali, and Senegal*
Jewelry and royal regalia primarily made by the Akan-speaking peoples in the 19th and 20th centuries. Catalogue.

Sept. 1–Dec. 31
Allan McCollum Photography
The artist presents abstract views of society by enlarging small portions of photographs of television frames.

Sept. 1–Mar. 3, 1991
Rock Art Photographs
Images of the stone carvings of the Anasazi Indians.

Oct. 6–Dec. 2
Chinese Snuff Bottles from the Pamela R. Lessing-Friedman Collection
Snuff bottles in jade, precious stones, and metals.

Oct. 13–Jan. 6, 1991
Frank Lloyd Wright: Preserving an Architectural Heritage
Examines Wright's concept of organic architecture. Catalogue.

Des Moines, Iowa

Oct. 27–Feb. 3, 1991
Steina and Woody Vasulka: Video
Installation explores properties inherent in video technology.

Permanent Collection
Comprehensive holdings of ancient to contemporary art. African, Oceanic, Northwest Coast, North American Indian, Eskimo arts, featuring masks, rugs, totemic art, basketry, pottery; Latin American art, including Mexican Tarascan house, Duran Chapel—complete with santos—Peruvian religious art; Asian art, including outstanding Indian collection; Renaissance and baroque painting; 19th- and early 20th-century painting; period rooms of English Tudor, Spanish baroque, French Gothic styles; art of the American West; Neusteter Gallery of costumes and textiles.
Highlights: American furniture; Degas, *The Dance Examination;* Grooms, *William Penn Shaking Hands with the Indians;* Monet, *The Water Lily Pond.* **Architecture:** 1971 building by Ponti and Sudler.

Admission
Adults $3; seniors & students $1.50; children under 5 free. Sat., free.

Hours
Tues.–Sat., 10–5; Sun., noon–5. Closed Mon. & holidays.

Tours
Mon.–Thurs., 1–4. Call (303) 575-2007.

Food & Drink
Café: Tues.–Sat., 11–2.

Des Moines Art Center

**4700 Grand Ave., Des Moines, Iowa 50312
(515) 277-4405**

1990 Exhibitions
Thru Jan. 28
David Dunlap

Thru Jan. 28
Renaissance Manuscripts and Prints

Feb. 17–Apr. 8
Mark Gordon: Artist-in-Residence
Features recent large-scale work in clay.

Feb. 17–Apr. 8
Print Shows/Works on Paper

Feb. 7–Apr. 8
T. L. Solien
Retrospective of 44 paintings, prints, pastels.

Des Moines, Iowa

Apr. 27–June 23
Emilio Ambasz: Architecture, Exhibition, Industrial, and Graphic Design
A comprehensive retrospective by one of this century's most influential architects and designers.

Apr. 28–June 17
Bill Viola
Video installations.

Apr. 28–June 17
Jack Wilkes: Artist-in-Residence
Recent paintings.

Apr. 28–June 17
Print Shows/Works on Paper

July 14–Aug. 26
Iowa Artists 1990
An all-media juried exhibition.

July 28–Sept. 23
Richard Diebenkorn: The "Forty-one Etchings Drypoints" Portfolio
Features a suite of 41 etchings and drypoints produced by Crown Point Press.

Sept. 15–Oct. 28
Lewis Baltz
Surveys the midcareer work of the noted California photographer.

Nov. 17–Jan. 13, 1991
Joel Shapiro: Figurative Sculpture
Features about 20 works from the 1970s to the present.

Wall Drawing #601– Forms Derived from a Cube, by Sol LeWitt. Des Moines Art Center.

Permanent Collection
Fine 19th- and 20th-century European and American paintings and sculptures; African and primitive arts. **Highlights:** Palace door by the Nigerian artist Arowogun of Osi; Bacon, *Study after Velázquez's "Portrait of Pope Innocent X"*; Johns, *Tennyson;* Judd, *Untitled;* Kiefer, *Untitled;* Monet, *Rocks at Belle-Ile;* Macdonald-Wright, *Abstraction on Spectrum.* **Architecture:** 1948 building by Eliel Saarinen; 1968 addition by Pei; 1985 building by Meier.

Admission
Free. Entrance fee for selected exhibitions. Handicapped accessible.

Hours
Tues.–Sat., 11–5; Thurs., 11–9; Sun., noon–5. Closed Mon. & holidays.

Tours
Sun. at 2. Call (515) 277-4405, ext. 32.

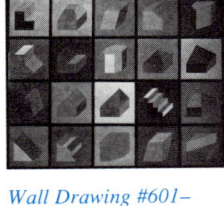

Detroit, Mich.

Food & Drink
Restaurant: Tues.–Sat., 11–3; Thurs. dinner, 5:30–9; Sun., noon–4.

The Detroit Institute of Arts

**5200 Woodward Ave., Detroit, Mich. 48202
(313) 833-7900**

1990 Exhibitions
Thru Jan. 28
Holy Image, Holy Space: Icons and Frescoes from Greece
Features about 80 early Byzantine works gathered from all over Greece. Catalogue.

Thru Jan. 28
OMAP IX
An ongoing Michigan Artist Program exhibition.

Thru Feb. 4
Site and Self: Nineteenth-Century French Landscapes, Prints, and Drawings from the Permanent Collection and Detroit-Area Collections
Celebrates the bicentennial of the French Revolution.

Thru Feb. 4
Wendell Castle Retrospective
Surveys the work of the contemporary American sculptor who challenges traditional concepts of furniture design. Catalogue.

Jan. 16–Mar. 11
Pierre Dubreuil Rediscovered: Masterprints, 1900–1935
Retrospective of one of photography's first modernists.

Mar. 11–Apr. 29
Fragile Memories: The Jerome Smith Collection of Staffordshire Figurines, 1760–1900
Some 65 English figurines, once used as mantlepieces, depict a cross-section of Georgian and Victorian interests.

Mar. 20–June 3
Dubuffet Prints from the Museum of Modern Art
Retrospective features 70 prints by the renowned French sculptor, painter, and printmaker.

Mar. 27–May 27
†*American Paintings from the Manoogian Collection*
Nineteenth-century works by Bierstadt, Bingham, Cropsey, Eakins, Heade. Catalogue.

April
Fifty-third Annual Detroit Public Schools Exhibition

Detroit, Mich.

Apr. 3–June 24
Recent Acquisitions: Photography

May 27–July 29
Andy Warhol: Fifteen Minutes of Fame
Portraits on paper and canvas by the American pop artist.

June 24–Sept. 2
†*Helen Frankenthaler: A Painting Retrospective*
Traces the renowned American artist's career over the past four decades. Catalogue.

July 10–Sept. 2
Picturing California
Surveys creative landscape photography from daguerreotypes of the 1850s to recent avant-garde images.

Sept. 8–Nov. 4
Wu Guanzhong
Features paintings superbly synthesizing eastern and western stylistic elements by a contemporary Beijing artist who studied Western methods in Paris in the 1940s.

Oct.–Jan., 1991
American and European Prints from the Schwartz Collection

Nov. 10–Dec. 30
Life through the Sixties
Photographs selected from the archives of *Life* magazine.

Dec. 9–Feb. 17, 1991
†*Gari Melchers: A Retrospective*
First significant exhibition since 1938 of the work of the famed Detroit artist. Catalogue.

Permanent Collection
Extensive holdings of African and Native American arts; European and American painting from the Middle Ages to the present; decorative arts; graphic arts; theater arts; textiles; oriental and Near Eastern art; 20th-century decorative arts and design; period rooms. **Highlights:** Brueghel, *Wedding Dance;* Caravaggio, *Conversion of the Magdalen;* Degas, *Violinist and Young Woman;* van Eyck, *Saint Jerome in His Study;* Picasso, *Bather by the Sea;* Rembrandt, *The Visitation;* Whistler, *Arrangement in Gray: Portrait of the Painter* and *Nocturne in Black and Gold: The Falling Rocket;* German expressionist paintings by Kirchner, Klee, Nolde; courtyard with Rivera's Detroit Industry frescoes.
Architecture: 1924 Italianate building by Cret.

Admission
Free; donations suggested. Handicapped accessible.

Hours
Tues.–Sun., 9:30–5:30. Closed Mon. & holidays.

Tours
Tues.–Sat. at 12:15; Sun. at 1 & 2:30. Tours of special exhibitions available.

Food & Drink
Kresge Court Café: Tues–Sat., 11–4; Sun., 1–4. La Palette Dining Room: Tues.–Fri., 11:30–2.

Museum of Art, Fort Lauderdale

One East Las Olas Blvd., Fort Lauderdale, Fla. 33301
(305) 525-5500; 763-6464 (recorded)

1990 Exhibitions
Indefinite
Alechinsky Works on Paper
A selection of works by the contemporary Belgian master from the permanent collection.

Thru Jan. 7
The Holiday Show
Celebrates holiday customs from many cultures; includes costumes, toys, tableaus, and a multimedia presentation.

Thru Jan. 30
David Stromeyer Sculptures
Presents three large, colorfully painted steel sculptures by the nationally known abstractionist.

Thru Feb. 11
African, South Pacific Islands, American Indian, and Pre-Columbian Art from the Permanent Collection
About 300 masterworks including wood and stone sculpture, modeled earthenware, metalwork, jewelry, textiles.

Jan. 26–Mar. 25
Masterpieces of American Illustration from the Delaware Art Museum
Includes original drawings and paintings later reproduced in books, magazines, and newpapers by artists Luks, Parrish, Pyle, N. C. and Andrew Wyeth.

Jan. 26–Mar. 25
Masterworks of Italian Paintings from the Ringling Museum
Includes works by masters Bassano, Canaletto, Cavaliere, di Cosimo, Luini, Pordenone, Salviati.

Jan. 31–Mar. 18
Video Paintings by Suzanne Giroux
Features a series of small nude and landscape images created by projecting video images onto a canvas that has been coated with gesso.

Fort Lauderdale, Fla.

Feb. 6–May
John Chamberlain—Sculpture
Displays large abstract sculptures created since the mid-50s.

Feb. 27–Apr. 29
Wolf Kahn Paintings
A selection of 30 paintings by the American impressionist.

Feb. 27–July 31
Prints from the Permanent Collection
Includes works by Calder, Close, Marini, Rivers, Warhol.

Mar. 23–May 20
"Best of the Eighties" by Craig Rubadoux
Drawings and paintings by the Florida artist.

Apr. 13–July 31
The Boat Show: Fantastic Vessels, Fictional Voyages
Three-dimensional objects in materials from marble to straw by 16 contemporary artists draw upon the legacy of maritime imagery and symbolism.

Apr. 13–July 31
Photographs by Stanley Rosenfield
Features works by the world-renowned boat photographer to coincide with the international Whitbread Race.

May 25–July 31
Mary Peck: Photographic Series on Florida Everglades
Images by the noted Santa Fe photographer.

Permanent Collection
European and American art with emphasis on the 20th century; impressive holdings of COBRA paintings, sculptures, prints; Oceanic, West African, Pre-Columbian, American Indian art; regional art. **Highlights:** Appel, *Personality;* Frankenthaler, *Nature Abhors a Vacuum;* Glackens, *Cape Cod Pier;* Warhol, *Mick Jagger*.
Architecture: 1986 building by Barnes.

Admission
Adults $3.25; seniors $2.75; students with ID $1.25; members & children under 12 free. Groups of 10 or more $2.75 per person. Handicapped accessible; wheelchairs available.

Hours
Tues., 11–9; Wed.–Sat., 10–5; Sun., noon–5. Closed Mon. & holidays.

Tours
Tues. at noon & 6:30; Wed.–Fri. at noon; Sat.–Sun. at 2.

Fort Worth, Tex.

Amon Carter Museum

**3501 Camp Bowie Blvd., Fort Worth, Tex. 76107
(817) 738-1933**

1990 Exhibitions

Thru Jan. 14
Eyewitness to War: Prints and Daguerreotypes of the Mexican War, 1846–1848
The Mexican War was the first military conflict to be photographed by eyewitness journalists and field artists; exhibition includes original daguerreotypes. Catalogue.

Thru Feb. 18
American Prints: Recent Acquisitions
Features color woodcuts by Dow, Nordfeldt, Weber and early modernist prints by Dreier, Spruance, Storrs.

Jan. 20–Mar. 18
Robert Adams: To Make It Home: Photographs of the American West
Noted landscape photographer juxtaposes the natural beauty and vastness of the West with society's encroachment on the once unspoiled environment. Catalogue.

Feb. 23–Apr. 22
Visual Poetry: The Drawings of Joseph Stella
Offers insights into the romantic, symbolist, and mystical aspects of Stella's creative expression. Catalogue.

Mar. 24–May 20
†*Worthington Whittredge*
Paintings of the Hudson River school artist reveal the evolution of his career and reflect the course of American landscape painting. Catalogue.

Apr. 27–June 24
Of Time and Place: Walker Evans and William Christenberry
Images depict the photographers' perspectives of Alabama, particularly in 1936 tenant farming families that were the subject of Evans and Agee's "Let Us Now Praise Famous Men" and a return trip made by Evans with Christenberry in 1973. Catalogue.

May 26–July 22
Training Hand and Eye: American Drawings from the Cooper-Hewitt
Features 19th- and 20th-century landscapes, figure studies, and illustrations by Church, Gibson, Homer, Moran, Richards, Sloan.

June 29–Aug. 26
Clara Sipprell
Delicate, light-infused still lifes, landscapes, and sensitive portraits of leading figures such as Stieglitz and Robert Frost by the noted contemporary photographer. Catalogue.

Mother and Daughter, Both Wearing Large Hats, 1900–01, by Mary Cassatt. Amon Carter Museum.

Fort Worth, Tex.

July 28–Sept. 23
A Spectrum of Innovation: Color in American Printmaking, 1890–1960
First survey of the history in the U.S. of fine-art color printmaking; includes woodcuts, lithographs, and etchings by Baumann, Cassatt, Davis, Roszak. Catalogue.

Sept. 29–Nov. 25
George N. Barnard: Photographer of Sherman's Campaign
Surveys Barnard's images of Civil War and plantation life, early daguerreotype portraits, and stereographs of the Chicago fire ruins of 1871.

Dec. 1–Feb. 3, 1991
Mark Klett: Colorado River Photographs
Images of the Grand Canyon taken over the past decade reveal the artist's highly personal and modern perspective. Catalogue.

Permanent Collection
Art of the American West, including work by Remington and Russell; 19th- and 20th-century painting, sculpture, graphic art by Davis, Demuth, Harnett, Homer, Marin, Nadelman, O'Keeffe. **Highlights:** Comprehensive collection of American photography; Heade, *Thunderstorm over Narragansett Bay;* Lane, *Boston Harbor;* Remington, *A Dash for the Timber*. **Architecture:** 1961 building by Johnson.

Admission
Free. Handicapped accessible.

Hours
Tues.–Sat., 10–5; Sun., 1–5:30. Closed Mon., Jan. 1, July 4, Thanksgiving, Dec. 25.

Tours
Tues.–Sun. at 2. For group reservations call (817) 738-6811.

Kimbell Art Museum

3333 Camp Bowie Blvd., Fort Worth, Tex. 76107-2744
(817) 332-8451

1990 Exhibitions
Thru Jan. 14
Style and Expressionism in Modern Chinese Painting: Robert Hatfield Ellsworth Collection at the Metropolitan Museum of Art
Features over 80 Chinese paintings from the late 19th century to the present.

Thru Jan. 21
The Consul Smith Collection: Raphael to Canaletto
Presents 60 masterpiece drawings from Windsor Castle.

Fort Worth, Tex.

Thru Mar. 18
†*Imperial Taste: Chinese Ceramics from the Percival David Foundation*
Includes 56 stunning ceramics collected by Chinese emperors of the Ming, Qing, Song, and Yuan dynasties from the Percival David collection of 1,400 ceramic works.

Jan. 27–Mar. 25
†*Expressionism and Modern German Painting from the Thyssen-Bornemisza Collection*
Works from the distinguished family collection focusing on the movements of the Brück, Blaue Reiter, Bauhaus, and Neue Sachlichkeit. Includes works by Kandinsky, Kirchner, and Nolde. Catalogue.

Apr. 7–June 17
The Art Museums of Louis I. Kahn
First in-depth analysis of the architect's projects, featuring 120 drawings and five models. Catalogue.

Aug. 18–Oct. 21
Five Centuries of Master Drawings from the Museum Boymans-van Beuningen, Rotterdam
Features the finest 15th- to 19th-century drawings from the museum's renowned collection; includes drawings by Breughel, Delacroix, Dürer, van Eyck, Fragonard, Goya, Ingres, Rembrandt, Rubens, Tintoretto, Van Dyck.

Permanent Collection
European painting and sculpture through the early 20th century; Asian paintings, sculptures, ceramics; Mesoamerican, African, ancient Mediterranean art. **Highlights:** Caravaggio, *Cardsharps;* Cézanne, *Man in a Blue Smock;* Duccio, *Raising of Lazarus;* Fra Angelico, *Saint James Freeing Hermogenes;* La Tour, *Cheat with the Ace of Clubs;* Mantegna, *Holy Family with Saint Elizabeth and the Infant Saint John the Baptist;* Mondrian, *Composition No. 7 (Facade);* Monet, *Pointe de la Heve at Low Tide;* Picasso, *Man With a Pipe* and *Nude Combing Her Hair;* Poussin, *Venus and Adonis;* Rembrandt, *Portrait of a Young Jew;* Rubens, *The Duke of Buckingham;* Ruisdael, *A Stormy Sea;* Titian, *Madonna and Child with Saint Catherine and the Infant Saint John the Baptist.* **Architecture:** 1967–72 building by Kahn, set in a park environment with reflecting pools.

Admission
Free. Handicapped accessible.

Hours
Tues.–Sat., 10–5; Sun., 11–5. Closed Mon. & holidays.

Tours
Sun. at 3. Selected exhibitions: Tues.–Fri. & Sun. at 2. For group tour reservations call (817) 738-6811.

Food & Drink
Buffet Restaurant: Tues.–Sat., 11:30–4; Sun., noon–4. Reservations recommended, call (817) 332-8451.

The Cardsharps, (I Bari), c. 1594–95, by Michelangelo Merisi da Caravaggio. Kimbell Art Museum.

Fort Worth, Tex.

Modern Art Museum of Fort Worth

1309 Montgomery St., Fort Worth, Tex. 76107
(817) 738-9215

1990 Exhibitions
Thru Jan. 7
†*Helen Frankenthaler: A Painting Retrospective*
Traces the renowned American artist's career over the past four decades. Catalogue.

Feb. 11–Apr. 8
Vernon Fisher
Features free-standing sculptures, wall pieces, and works on paper, exhibiting Fisher's witty, mordantly literal fusion of language and visual imagery. Catalogue.

Permanent Collection
Comprehensive collection of contemporary art with works by Bartlett, Benglis, Graves, Grosz, Hockney, Hodgkin, Hofmann, Kelly, Klee, Louis, Motherwill, Olitski, Pollock, Rauschenberg, Stella, Sultan, Weber. **Highlights:** Eakins, *The Swimming Hole;* Inness, *Approaching Storm;* Judd, *Untitled;* Kandinsky, *Above and Left;* Kelly, *Curved Red on Blue;* Picasso, *Suite Vollard, Reclining Woman Reading, Head of a Woman;* Rothko, *Light Cloud, Dark Cloud;* Still, *Untitled.* **Architecture:** 1901 gallery; 1954 first museum building by Bayer; 1974 addition with garden courtyard and solarium by Ford & Associates.

Admission
Free. Handicapped accessible.

Hours
Tues.–Sat., 10–5; Sun., 1–5. Closed Mon., and holidays.

Tours
For group tour reservations call (817) 738-6811.

Hood Museum of Art

Dartmouth College, Hanover, N.H. 03755
(603) 646-2808

1990 Exhibitions
Thru Feb. 25
**Ellsworth Kelly: A Print Retrospective*
Emphasizes the work produced by the American artist at Gemini G.E.L. and Tyler Graphics; includes a selection of handmade-paper prints of the mid-1970s. Catalogue.

Hanover, N.H.

Feb. 24–May 13
"Lessons Stitched in Silk": Samplers from the Canterbury Region of New Hampshire
Examines their role in early 19th-century New England public education.

Mar. 10–May 20
By Good Hands: New Hampshire Folk Art
Catalogue.

May 26–July 1
CLICK! 1900–1990
Features American and European photographs; includes portraits, landscapes, and examples of photojournalism, abstraction, and manipulated imagery.

June 9–Aug. 26
The Garden Paintings: Recent Work by Thomas George
Paintings and pastels created during visits to European gardens.

July 14–Sept. 2
Regional Selections 1990

Aug. 25–Oct. 21
The Artful Line: Contemporary Abstract Drawings from Private Collections
Thirty drawings by Dunham, Hesse, Lewett, Serra, Shapiro, Winters, and others.

Sept. 15–Dec. 9
Fatal Consequences
War prints by Callot and Goya address the tragedy and carnage of warfare. Catalogue.

Oct. 27–Dec. 16
Where War Lives: A Photographic Journal by Dick Durrance
Images by the Vietnam Army photographer taken 1966–68 convey the brutality and poignancy of the Vietnam experience. Catalogue.

Panathenaic Amphora, c. 500–475 B.C., The Berlin Painter, Greece. Hood Museum of Art.

Permanent Collection
American art and silver including works by Copley, Eakins, Revere, Whistler; European paintings, sculptures, and graphics by Dürer, Picasso, Pissaro, Titian. Chinese bronzes and ceramics; Pre-Columbian, Oceanic, African art; Native American art. **Highlights:** Assyrian reliefs; Panathenaic amphora by the Berlin painter; Orozco murals; Eakins, *Portrait of John Joseph Borie;* Picasso, *Guitar on the Table;* Revere and other American silver. **Architecture:** 1985 building by Moore and Floyd of Centerbrook Architects.

Admission
Free. Handicapped accessible.

Hartford, Conn.

Hours
Tues.–Fri. & Sun., 11–5; Sat., 11–8. Closed Mon., Jan. 1, Dec. 24–25.

Tours
Wed. at 12:30; Sat.–Sun. at 2. Call (603) 646-2010.

Wadsworth Atheneum

600 Main St., Hartford, Conn. 06103
(203) 278-2670; 247-9111 (recorded)

1990 Exhibitions
Jan. 14–Apr. 15
Tim Rollins and K.O.S./Matrix 109
Large-scale works incorporating literary themes from texts by Crane, Kafka, Orwell, and others by Rollins and K.O.S., Kids of Survival, a group of South Bronx teenage students.

Saint Serapion, 1628, by Francisco de Zurbarán. Wadsworth Atheneum.

Jan. 28–Mar. 25
From Vasari to Stella: Master Drawings from the Wadsworth Atheneum
Includes works by artists ranging from the 16th-century by biographer Vasari to Rembrandt pupils Bol and Maes; Venetian artists Piazzetta and Tiepolo; 19th-century French artists Courbet and Daumier; pre-Raphaelites including Hunt; 20th-century masters Klee, Miró, Moore, Picasso.

Mar. 18–Apr. 15
Winslow Homer
Features watercolors and oil paintings from the 1860s and 1870s, including *The Berry Pickers.*

Mar. 18–May 20
†*John Twachtman: Connecticut Landscapes*
Works by one of the most admired American impressionist painters, best known for the subtle and poetic qualities of his landscapes.

June 9–Sept. 2
Robert Longo
Documents the thematic development of the artist's work, from his early performance pieces to his current monumental reliefs and constructions. Catalogue.

Permanent Collection
Greek and Roman bronzes, baroque art, American paintings, French and German porcelains, early American furniture, 20th-century masterpieces. **Highlights:** Caravaggio, *Ecstasy of Saint Francis;* landscapes by Church and Cole; Goya, *Gossiping Women;* Pollock, *Number 9;* Rembrandt, *Portrait of a Young Man;* Renoir, *Monet Painting in His Garden at Argenteuil;* Zurburán, *Saint Serapion;* Trumbull's painting of Daniel Wadsworth and his father. **Architecture:** 1844 Neo-Gothic Wadsworth building by Davis; 1907

Tudor-style Colt Memorial; 1907 Renaissance-revival Morgan Memorial; 1934 Avery Memorial with International-style interior; 1969 Goodwin building.

Admission
Adults $3; seniors & students $1.50; members & children under 13, Thurs., free. Sat., 11–1, free. Handicapped accessible.

Hours
Tues.–Sun., 11–5. Closed Mon. & holidays.

Tours
Thurs. & Sat.–Sun. at 1. Call (203) 278-2670, ext. 323.

Food & Drink
Museum Café: Tues.–Fri., 11:30–2:30; Sat.–Sun., noon–3.

Honolulu Academy of Arts

900 South Beretania St., Honolulu, Hawaii 96814
(808) 538-3693

1990 Exhibitions
Thru Jan. 7
In Pursuit of the Dragon: Traditions and Transitions in Ming Ceramics
Presents exceptional Chinese porcelainware dating from the 14th to the 17th century. Catalogue.

Jan. 4–Feb. 11
Jimmy Pike Graphics
New works by the Australian aborigine artist.

Jan. 25–Mar. 4
A Golden Age of Painting: Sixteenth- and Seventeenth-Century Dutch, Flemish, and German Paintings from the Sarah Campbell Blaffer Foundation
An exhibition of major works.

Jan. 25–Mar. 4
Robert Stackhouse
Features large watercolors and sculptures by the New York-based contemporary artist.

Feb. 20–Mar. 25
The Board Room
Presents a controversial video installation by Spanish-born artist Muntadas.

Feb. 27–Apr. 8
Cox Prize Exhibition: Dorothy Faison
Features new works on paper by the Honolulu artist, winner of the Cox Prize.

Houston, Tex.

Mar. 22–May 6
Georgia O'Keeffe: Paintings of Hawaii
Features 20 works painted during O'Keeffe's visit to Hawaii in the 1930s.

Mar. 22–May 6
Parallels and Contrasts: Photographs from the Stephen White Collection
An exhibition of 19th- and 20th-century photographs exploring landscape, architecture, portraiture, the nude, and industrial and scientific subjects.

May 24–July 1
The Mirror: The Art of the Bronze Caster in Ancient China

May 24–July 1
Okinawan Artifacts from the Prefectural Museum of Naha, Okinawa

Nov. 29–Jan. 6, 1991
Artists of Hawaii 1990
Annual juried exhibition of contemporary Hawaiian art.

Permanent Collection
Hawaii's only general art museum with objects from cultures around the world and throughout history. Asian art, including Michener collection of Japanese prints; Kress collection of Renaissance and baroque paintings; American paintings and decorative arts; works from Africa, Oceania, the Americas; contemporary graphic arts. **Highlights:** Delauney, *The Rainbow;* van Gogh, *Wheatfields;* Ma Fen, *The Hundred Geese;* Monet, *Water Lilies;* Chinese and Persian bronzes; six garden courts. **Architecture:** 1927 building by Goodhue.

Admission
Free. Handicapped accessible.

Hours
Tues.–Sat., 10–4:30; Sun., 1–5. Closed Mon. & holidays.

Tours
Tues.–Wed. & Fri.–Sat. at 11; Thurs. & Sun. at 2.

Food & Drink
Garden Café: Tues.–Fri., 11:30–2. Thurs. dinner, 6:15. For reservations call (808) 531-8865.

Houston, Tex.

Contemporary Arts Museum

5216 Montrose Blvd. at Bissonnet, Houston, Tex. 77006-6598
(713) 526-0773; 526-3129 (recorded)

1990 Exhibitions
Thru Feb. 4
†*German Art of the Late Eighties*
Features works in a wide range of media by 26 young West German artists who explore relations between image, object, space, and text.

Jan. 13–Mar. 25
Terry Berkowitz: When the World Was Flat
An installation of video, sound, and objects address the sources of societal pressure—media and advertising, fashion and ideology—causing conformitites and loss of identity.

Feb. 24–May 20
Ida Applebroog: Happy Families
Features 70 early books, videotapes, and recent paintings in a major retrospective by the American artist. Catalogue.

Apr. 7–June 17
Benito Huerta: Attempted, Not Known
New works by the noted Texan artist, including large-scale paintings combining a wide variety of media and objects, works on paper, and a hand-colored book.

June 9–Aug. 19
Revered Earth
New works by contemporary artists whose concern with the environment has been a lifelong theme; includes large-scale installations. Catalogue.

June 30–Sept. 9
The International Pinhole Photography Exhibition
Includes 140 images, ten pinhole cameras, documentary photos of other cameras. Catalogue.

Permanent Collection
No permanent collection. **Architecture:** 1972 stainless-steel parallelogram building by Birkerts and Associates.

Admission
Donation suggested: $2. Handicapped accessible.

Hours
Tues.–Sat., 10–5; Sun., noon–6. Closed Mon., Jan. 1, July 4, Thanksgiving, Dec. 25.

Tours
Lower Perspectives Gallery, Sun. at 2; Upper Gallery at 3. Group tours available Tues. & Thurs. For reservations call (713) 526–0788.

Houston, Tex.

The Menil Collection

1515 Sul Ross, Houston, Tex. 77006
(713) 525-9400

1990 Exhibitions
Thru Mar. 4
Cy Twombly

Feb. 15–Mar. 31
Mark Riboud Photographs

Apr. 15–June 26
Jay De Feo
Displays 50 abstract works on paper in various media including graphite, charcoal, oil, pastel, collage. Catalogue.

Apr. 26–Sept. 8
The Birth of Venus: Neolithic and Chalcolithic Antiquities from Cyprus

Fall
Robert Rauschenberg: The Early Work from 1949 to 1955

Statue of Eannatum, Prince of Lagash, Summerian, 2600–2450 B.C., Southern Iraq. The Menil Collection.

Permanent Collection
Antiquities including Cycladic, Hellenistic, Roman, European artifacts; Byzantine icons; medieval art; art of tribal cultures featuring extensive surveys of African and Oceanic cultures; 20th-century works with particular strengths in cubism, surrealism, and abstract expressionism; Richmond Hall (1416 Richmond) presenting contemporary and experimental art and performance. **Highlights:** Sumerian statue of the Prince of Lagash; Ernst, *Day and Night;* Johns, *Voice;* Leger, *Still Life.* **Architecture:** 1987 building by Piano in association with Fitzgerald and Partners.

Admission
Free. Handicapped accessible.

Hours
Wed.–Sun., 11–7. Closed Mon.–Tues. & holidays.

The Museum of Fine Arts, Houston

1001 Bissonnet St., Houston, Tex. 77005
(713) 639-7300

1990 Exhibitions
Thru Jan. 7
†*Czech Modernism: 1900–1945*
Presents the evolution of the Czech avant-garde from expressionism through surrealism; focuses on the

Houston, Tex.

interdisciplinary aspects of painting, sculpture, works on paper, photography, film. Catalogue.

Thru Jan. 21
Containers and Vessels
A selection from the permanent collection.

Thru Jan. 28
†*The Intimate Interiors of Edouard Vuillard*
Paintings from the 1890s by the postimpressionist master who was a founder of the Nabis, an offshoot of the symbolist movement. Catalogue.

Feb. 4–Apr. 15
Money Matters: A Critical Look at Bank Architecture
The first major photographic survey of the history of bank architecture in the U.S. and Canada. Catalogue.

Feb. 25–Apr. 29
†*Pierre Bonnard: The Graphic Works*
Celebrates the artist's vision of everyday life; includes prints, drawings, illustrated books, oil paintings. Catalogue.

May 27–Aug. 19
Odyssey: The Art of Photography at the National Geographic
Depicts the development and expansion of the Society's photographic activity since the 1890s. Catalogue.

June 17–Aug. 19
Jasper Johns: Printed Symbols
Retrospective of the career of a major American artist— from *Target,* his first black-and-white lithography (1960), to multicolored etchings (1987). Catalogue.

Fall
On the Edge of the Maya World: Stone Vases from the Ulua Valley
An exhibition of travertine vases (A.D. 850–950) from the Ulua Valley of northwestern Honduras and 12 related objects. Catalogue.

Oct. 7–Dec. 30
Douglas Cooper: Collecting Cubism
Cubist collages from the estate of the late scholar and noted art critic, including Picasso's early cubist studies to works reflecting developments in Paris and outside France after World War I. Catalogue.

Dec. 2–Jan. 27, 1991
The Drawings of Adolph Menzel
About 100 works by the German artist (1815–1905) considered by many the greatest naturalist since Dürer. Catalogue.

Ithaca, N.Y.

Dec. 9–Mar. 17, 1991
The Sculpture of Indonesia
Exhibits 120 works from the Neolithic period to the 13th century, including stone and bronze sculptures, metalwork, and works from 9th-century Borobudur in Java. Catalogue.

Permanent Collection
Works ranging from ancient to modern: Straus collection of Renaissance and 18th-century art; Beck collection of impresionist and postimpressionist art; Target collection of American photography. **Highlights:** Greek bronze Youth; Bayou Bend collection of 17th- to 19th-century furniture, silver, ceramics, paintings; Brancusi, *A Muse;* Cézanne, *Portrait of the Artist's Wife;* van Gogh, *The Rocks;* Pollock, *Number 6;* van der Weyden, *Virgin and Child;* Noguchi sculpture garden. **Architecture:** 1924 building by Watkin; 1926 east and west wings; 1958 and 1974 additions by Mies van der Rohe.

Admission
Adults $2; seniors & college students with ID $1; members & children under 18 free. Thurs., free. Handicapped accessible.

Hours
Tues.–Sat., 10–5; Thurs., 10–9; Sun., 12:15–6. Closed Mon. & major holidays.

Tours
Daily noon. For group tour reservations call (713) 639-7324.

Food & Drink
Museum Café: Tues.–Sat., 10–2; Thurs., 10–2 and 5–7; Sat., 10–4; Sun., 12:15–4.

Herbert F. Johnson Museum of Art

Cornell University, Ithaca, N.Y. 14853-4001
(607) 255-6464

1990 Exhibitions
Jan. 23–Mar. 11
Robert Cottingham: A Print Retrospective, 1972–1988
First major retrospective of an important photo-realist who works from slides and photos to compose sharply focused urban scenes.

Jan. 30–Mar. 25
Vanishing Presence
Displays 19th- and 20th-century photographs, time exposures, multiple exposures, blurred effects. Catalogue.

Jacksonville, Fla.

Mar. 16–May 6
Arthur Wesley Dow and His Influence
Explores Dow's work and focus as an orientalist who influenced Coburn, O'Keeffe, and Weber.

Apr. 3–May 29
Wu Guanzhong
Features paintings superbly synthesizing eastern and western stylistic elements by a contemporary Beijing artist who studied western methods in Paris in the 1940s.

Aug. 23–Nov. 4
125 Years of American Art from the Collections of Cornell Alumni and Friends

Nov. 13–Dec. 21
Photographs and Films by Johann van der Keuken
Works by the contemporary Dutch artist. Catalogue.

Permanent Collection
Paintings, sculptures, prints, drawings, photographs, crafts, textiles from 30 centuries and six continents with strengths in Asian and American art. **Highlights:** Daubigny, Fields in the Month of June; Durand, View of th*e Hudson Valley;* Giacometti, *Walking Man II;* Leoni, *Portrait of Angela Gratiani;* Russell, *Synchromy No. 5;* Stieglitz, *The Steerage;* Tiffany blue vase. **Architecture:** 1973 building by Pei.

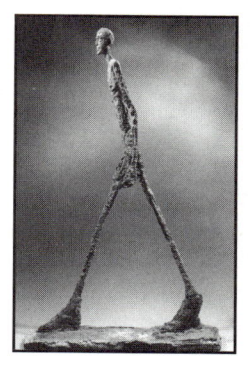

Walking Man II, by Alberto Giacometti. Herbert F. Johnson Museum of Art.

Admission
Free. Handicapped accessible; wheelchair available.

Hours
Tues.–Sun., 10–5. Closed Mon. & holidays.

Tours
Call (607) 255-6464.

Jacksonville Art Museum

4160 Boulevard Center Dr., Jacksonville, Fla. 32207
(904) 398-8336

1990 Exhibitions
Thru Jan. 7
*Focus on the Image: Selections from the Rivendell Collection
Includes drawings, paintings, photographs, and sculptures by major European and American artists who have recently gained prominence in the art world.

Feb. 1–Mar. 31
Young Americans
Features crafts by award-winning artists aged 18 to 30.

Kansas City, Mo.

Feb. 1–Apr. 30
Chinese Snuff Bottles
Features a collection of exquisite snuff bottles dating from 1650 to 1850.

May 31–Aug. 31
Jacksonville Creates
Drawings, paintings, photographs, and sculptures.

Sept. 6–Oct. 15
Made in Florida
Works by noted artists including Rauschenberg and Rosenquist.

Permanent Collection
Pre-Columbian artifacts; works by Florida artists; 20th-century American paintings, sculptures, prints featuring works by Frankenthaler, Katz, Nevelson, Stella. **Highlights:** Koger collection of oriental porcelains and ceramics; sculpture court. **Architecture:** 1966 building by Hardwick; 1973 Koger Gallery by Broward.

Admission
Free. Handicapped accessible.

Hours
Tues.–Fri., 10–4; Thurs., 10–10; Sat.–Sun., 1–5. Closed Mon. & holidays.

Tours
Call (904) 398-8336 for information.

The Nelson-Atkins Museum of Art

4525 Oak St., Kansas City, Mo. 64111
(816) 561-4000

1990 Exhibitions
Thru Jan. 28
Yani: The Brush of Innocence
Displays 69 works by the 14-year-old who began painting at the age of two and had her first exhibition at the age of four; includes many of her noted monkey paintings. Catalogue.

Jan. 19–Mar. 11
John Ahearn
Horizons series of contemporary art exhibitions.

Jan. 21–Feb. 25
Figuratively Speaking: Drawings by Seven Artists
Fifty-six drawings by Abakanowicz, Goodwin, Hunt, Penck, Roosen, Shea, and Walker redefine figurative presentation.

Kansas City, Mo.

Feb. 17–Mar. 25
The Ceramic Art of Joan Miró
The first museum exhibition of ceramics by the Spanish artist; includes plates, vases, plaques, large sculptural forms.

Apr. 6–June 3
Contemporary Illustrated Books: Word and Image, 1967–1987
Horizons series of contemporary art exhibitions.

Apr. 21–June 17
†*Impressionism: Selections from Five American Museums*
Features 85 paintings and sculptures by the celebrated impressionists and postimpressionists Bonnard, Cassatt, Degas, van Gogh, Manet, Monet, Pissarro, Renoir.

Apr. 29–June 3
Warrington Colescott: Forty Years of Printmaking

July 8–Sept. 2
Japonisme Comes to America, 1876–1925
In-depth exhibition shows the Japanese influence on turn-of-the-century graphic arts; includes works on paper by such artists as Coburn, Hyde, and La Farge.

July 15–Sept. 2
George N. Barnard: Photographer of Sherman's Campaign
Surveys Barnard's images of Civil War and plantation life, early daguerreotype portraits, and stereographs of the Chicago fire ruins of 1871.

July 22–Sept. 2
Drawings by Francesco and Giovanni Carlo Bibiena
Work of the 18th-century Florentine and Bolognese family of scenographic designers; includes drawings, engravings, books, manuscripts.

Oct. 7–Nov. 25
Jacques Lipchitz: A Retrospective
Features the Lithuanian-born artist's openwork sculpture.

Oct. 14–Dec. 2
A Spectrum of Innovation: Color in American Printmaking, 1890–1960

Dec. 16–Feb. 10, 1991
The Modern Poster: The Museum of Modern Art
More than 300 posters from MOMA's collection by such artists as Bayer, Lissitzky, Rodchenko, Toulouse-Lautrec.

Permanent Collection
European and American paintings, sculptures, prints, decorative arts; American, Indian, Oceanic, Pre-Columbian art; renowned collection of oriental art. **Highlights:** Largest permanent U.S. display of Bentons; Bingham, *Canvasing for a Vote;* Caravaggio, *Saint John the Baptist;* Guercino, *Saint Luke Displaying a Painting of the Virgin;*

de Kooning, *Woman IV;* Moore sculpture garden; Poussin, *The Triumph of Bacchus;* Rembrandt, *Youth with a Black Cap;* Renoir, *The Large Bather.* **Architecture:** 1933 neoclassical building by Wight and Wight.

Admission
Adults $3; students & children, 6–18, $1; children under 6 free. Sat.,–Sun. permanent collection free. Handicapped accessible.

Hours
Tues.–Sat., 10–5; Sun., 1–5. Closed Mon., Jan. 1, July 4, Thanksgiving, Dec. 24–25.

Tours
Tues.–Sat. at 10:30, 11, 1, 2; Sun. at 1:30, 2, 2:30, 3. Call (816) 561-4000, ext. 227.

Food & Drink
Rozelle Court Restaurant: Tues.–Sat., 10:30–4; Sun., 1–4.

La Jolla Museum of Contemporary Art

700 Prospect St., La Jolla, Calif. 92037
(619) 454-0267; 454-3541

1990 Exhibitions

Thru Jan. 7
Poster Art of the Soviet Union
Contemporary posters shown outside the USSR for the first time.

Thru Jan. 7
Robert Moskowitz, 1959–1989
Retrospective of the contemporary American artist who gained recognition with the "new image" painters of the 1970s.

Jan. 12–Apr. 1
Alfredo Jaar
A blend of architecture, photography, and theater address personal, political, and aesthetic issues. Catalogue.

Jan. 12–Apr. 1
The Medical Illustrations of Dr. Frank Netter
Works by the prolific illustrator known for his precise, imaginitive portrayals of the human system.

Apr. 6–June 3
Responses: Ann Hamilton, Maurizio Pellegrin, and Markus Raetz
Works made in response to the physical, geographical, and historical aspects of the museum.

Red Mill, 1981, by Robert Moskowitz. From *Robert Moskowitz* at La Jolla Museum of Contemporary Art, thru Jan. 7.

Lawrence, Kans.

June 8–Aug. 5
Satellite Intelligence: Boston/San Diego New Art Exchange
Works by ten emerging artists from each city. Catalogue.

Aug. 18–Oct. 14
Diamonds Are Forever: Artists and Writers on Baseball
Features paintings, photographs, and drawings that reflect on baseball as a national inspiration.

Permanent Collection
Twentieth-century holdings, spanning a variety of media with particularly strong minimalist, pop, postmodern work. **Highlights:** André, *Magnesium-Zinc Plain;* Kelly, *Red Blue Green;* Kirchner, *Self-Portrait with Model;* Oldenburg, *Alphabet, Good Humor;* Warhol, *Flowers.* **Architecture:** 1916 building by Gill; 1959, 1979 expansions by Mosher; 1991–92 renovation by Venturi planned.

Admission
Adults $3; seniors & students $1; children, 5–12, 50¢; children under 5 free. Wed., 5–9, free. Handicapped accessible.

Hours
Tues.–Sun., 10–5; Wed., 10–9. Closed Mon., holidays, 2d week of August.

Tours
Wed. at 12:30; Sat.–Sun. at 1:30 & 2:30.

Food & Drink
Sidewalk Café: Tues.–Sun., 11–3.

Spencer Museum of Art

University of Kansas, Lawrence, Kans. 66045
(913) 864-4710

1990 Exhibitions
Jan. 21–Mar. 4
Wu Guanzhong
Features paintings superbly synthesizing eastern and western stylistic elements by a contemporary Beijing artist who studied western methods in Paris in the 1940s.

Jan. 28–Mar. 1
The Healing Machines
Exhibition of "grassroots" art by a Nebraska farmer.

Mar. 25–May 6
Committed to Print
American prints address social and political concerns such as race and culture, gender, nuclear power and ecology, war and revolution, class struggle, and the American dream.

Los Angeles, Calif.

Mar. 25–May 20
The Prints of Richard Bosman
Features large blockprints on nautical themes by the contemporary American artist.

Sept. 23–Nov. 18
*I Dream a World: Portraits of Black Women Who Changed America
Seventy-five portraits by Pulitzer Prize winning photographer Brian Lanker of Maya Angelou, Shirley Chisholm, Odetta, Rosa Parks, Sarah Vaughn, and others. Catalogue.

Permanent Collection
Noted holdings of European painting and sculpture; American portrait and landscape paintings, prints, quilts, photographs; Edo period paintings; Korean ceramics; Japanese prints; contemporary Chinese painting. **Highlights:** Homer, *Cloud Shadows;* Claude Lorrain, *Landscape with a Draftsman;* Mitsuhiro, *Memoir from an Eastern Journey;* Riemen-schneider, *Virgin and Child;* Rossetti, *La Pia de' Tolommei;* Soldani, *Autumn and Summer;* Teniers, *The Deluge.* **Architecture:** 1978 building by Jenks.

Admission
Free. Handicapped accessible; wheelchairs available.

Hours
Tues.–Sat., 8:30–5; Sun., noon–5. Closed Mon., Jan. 1, July 4, Thanksgiving, Dec. 24–25.

Tours
Call (913) 864-4710 for information.

Los Angeles County Museum of Art

5905 Wilshire Blvd., Los Angeles, Calif. 90036
(213) 857-6111

1990 Exhibitions
Thru Feb. 18
The Paintings of Ito Jakuchu
First U.S. exhibition to feature one of the great painters in the history of Japanese art. Features scrolls, screens, panels, doors, books, prints, portraits. Catalogue.

Thru Feb. 25
On the Art of Fixing a Shadow: 150 Years of Art Photography
About 400 fine examples of photographic art produced since the invention of the medium in 1839. Catalogue.

Los Angeles, Calif.

Thru Mar. 11
†*The Romance of the Taj Mahal*
Presents the world-famous monument through models, prints, drawings, and paintings by Indian and British artists; also includes gems, jewelry, carpets, textiles. Catalogue.

Feb. 8–Apr. 22
†*Helen Frankenthaler: A Painting Retrospective*
Traces the renowned American artist's career over the past four decades. Catalogue.

Feb. 11–Apr. 29
†*Francis Bacon*
Surveys the achievement of the contemporary British painter, from his daring figure studies of the 1940s to very recent, vigorously inventive works. Catalogue.

Mar. 29–May 27
Callot to Piranesi: Old Master Prints from the Collection
Works on paper, including etchings, engravings, and woodcuts from the baroque and rococo periods by Callot, Canaletto, Piranesi, Rembrandt, Van Dyck.

Mar. 29–May 27
William Brice Notations, 1982
Pencil and color crayon drawings made on the back of 4 x 6 file cards feature forms, textures, and colors inspired by the California landscape.

Apr. 7–June 17
The Art of Van Cleef and Arpels
Jewelry and accessories from the 1920s–50s; features a variety of gems and settings displaying innovative techniques such as the "invisible setting" and the "minaudiere."

Apr. 19–June 24
Envisioning America: Prints, Drawings, and Photographs by George Grosz and His Contemporaries
Studies how American myths of the Wild West and the city influenced the art of the 1920s in Germany.

Apr. 29–Sept. 22
†*Thomas Hart Benton: An American Original*
Colorful and explosively energetic murals and easel paintings are featured in the first major retrospective of this famous American regionalist; held on the centennial of his birth. Catalogue.

May 10–July 15
The New Vision: Photography between the World Wars
Celebrates the 150th anniversary of photography with 115 vintage images illustrating the photographic revolution in 20th-century vision in Europe and America. Includes works by Abbott, Bayer, Brancusi, Bourke-White, Cartier-Bresson, Evans, Magritte, Man Ray, Rodchenko, Stieglitz, Weston. Catalogue.

New York Beauty, c. 1875, American. Los Angeles County Museum of Art.

Los Angeles, Calif.

June 17–Aug. 26
A Primal Spirit: Ten Contemporary Japanese Sculptors
Works created for the exhibition and selected earlier works. The art reinterprets traditional Japanese concepts about society's relationship to nature as well as the artist's response to profound cultural changes. Catalogue.

June 21–Sept. 9
Treasures from the Fitzwilliam Museum
Chosen from the extensive collection of the Fitzwilliam Museum of Cambridge University; includes paintings by Delacroix, Hals, Hogarth, Monet, Rubens, Titian, Van Dyke. Catalogue.

Aug. 16–Nov. 4
†*Masterpieces of Impressionism and Postimpressionism: The Annenberg Collection*
Formidable group of works by innovative 19th-century French artists; includes paintings by Cézanne, Gauguin, van Gogh, Monet, Renoir.

Oct. 7–Dec. 30
The Fauve Landscape

Permanent Collection
Ancient, Egyptian, Far Eastern, Indian, Southeast Asian art; Islamic art; Pre-Columbian Mexican pottery and textiles; European and American paintings, sculptures, prints, drawings, decorative arts; glass from antiquity to the present; costumes and textiles; photographs. **Highlights:** B. Gerald Cantor Sculpture Garden; Gilbert collection of mosaics and monumental gold and silver; Heeramaneck collection of art from India, Nepal, Tibet; de La Tour, *Magdalen with the Smoking Flame;* Matisse, *Tea;* Rodin bronzes.
Architecture: 1965 Ahmanson, Bing, and Hammer buildings by Pereira; 1986 Anderson building and central court by Hardy Holzman Pfeiffer Associates; 1988 Shin'enkan Pavilion for Japanese Art by Goff.

Admission
Adults $3; seniors & students with ID $1.50; children, 5–12, 75¢. Entrance fee for selected exhibitions. Handicapped accessible; wheelchairs available.

Hours
Tues.–Fri., 10–5; Sat.–Sun., 10–6. Closed Mon., Jan. 1, Thanksgiving, Dec. 25.

Tours
Call (213) 857-6108.

Food & Drink
Plaza Café in Leo S. Bing Center: Tues.–Fri., 10–4:30; Sat.–Sun., 10–5:30. Times Mirror Central Court Café (outdoors): Tues.–Sun., 11–5.

Los Angeles, Calif.

The Museum of Contemporary Art

MOCA at California Plaza
250 South Grand Ave., Los Angeles, Calif. 90012
(213) 621-2766

The Temporary Contemporary
152 North Central Ave., Los Angeles, Calif. 90013
(213) 621-2766

1990 Exhibitions
Thru Feb. 11 (Temporary Contemporary)
Blueprints for Modern Living: History and Legacy of the Case Study Houses
Includes about 30 scale models and two full-scale reconstructions of experimental houses built in Los Angeles, 1945–66. Catalogue.

Mar. 25–June 17
John Baldessari
A career survey of works by the influential Los Angeles artist-photographer, including his multilayered, postmodern narratives of image and text. Catalogue.

Apr. 1–June 24
Lothar Baumgarten
Images from the photographer's train trip across the U.S.

Apr. 22–June
Roni Horn
Five installations/sculptures by the New York artist.

Nov.–Jan. (The Temporary Contemporary)
The Independent Group: Postwar Britain and the Aesthetics of Plenty

Dec.–Jan., 1991 (California Plaza)
Edward Ruscha
Paintings since the late 1970s by the Los Angeles artist.

Personnages dans la nuit, 1949, by Joan Miró. The Museum of Contemporary Art.

Permanent Collection
Paintings, sculptures, photographs, performance works, and environmental works from the 1940s to the present.
Highlights: Heizer, *Double Negative;* Kline, *Black Iris;* Rauschenberg, *Interview;* Rothko, *Red & Brown;* Rothenberg, *The Hulk;* Ruscha, Annie; Syrop, *Treated and Released.* **Architecture:** 1983 Temporary Contemporary warehouse reno-vated by Gehry; 1986 California Plaza building by Isozaki.

Admission
Adults $4; seniors & students with ID $2; children under 12 free. Thurs., 5–8, free. Handicapped accessible.

Louisville, Ky.

Hours
Tues.–Wed. & Fri.–Sun., 11–6; Thurs., 11–8. Closed Mon., Jan. 1, Dec. 25.

Food & Drink
Il Panino (MOCA): Open during museum hours.

The J. B. Speed Art Museum

P.O. Box 2600
2035 South Third St., Louisville, Ky. 40201-2600
(502) 636-2893

1990 Exhibitions
Thru Jan. 7
The Appropriate Object
Features works by a group of contemporary black artists who work in similar materials; includes Hassinger, Hunt, Jackson, Loving, Saar, Saunders, Scott.

Thru Jan. 7
Black Art Anniversary Invitational

Thru Jan. 7
Houston Conwill: Art at the Edge
A small-scale installation that overlays the metaphor of the cakewalk slave dance with reference to the history and achievements of blacks in the South.

Mar. 13–indefinite
On Native Ground: Masterpieces from the J. B. Speed Art Museum's Native American Collection
Features objects from the Arapaho, Cheyenne, Oglala, Ojibwa, and Sioux nations.

Apr. 3–May 27
†*Of Time and the City: American Modernism, 1910–1930, Selections from the Sheldon Memorial Art Gallery*
Explores the response of American artists to European modernist ideas, particularly cubism and abstraction.

June 5–July 29
Circus and Sport: Staffordshire Figures, 1790–1840
Early ceramic art mirrors the customs, manners, and fascinations of the late 18th- and early 19th-century English rural society.

June 5–July 29
Majolica Ware from Southern Collections
About 50 objects illustrate the variety of technical effects and diversity of styles found in Italian majolica.

Permanent Collection
European and American paintings, sculptures, and prints from antiquity to the present; American Indian and oriental

art; 17th-century Dutch art; 18th-century French art; 20th-century sculpture and painting. **Highlights:** Elaborately carved oak-paneled English Renaissance room; sculpture garden; Brancusi, *Mlle Pogany;* Rubens, *The Triumph of the Eucharist.* **Architecture:** 1927 building modeled after The Cleveland Museum of Art; 1954 and 1973 wings; 1983 addition by Geddes.

Admission
Adults $2; seniors $1; members, students, children free. Sat., free. Handicapped accessible.

Hours
Tues.–Sat., 10–4; Sun., 1–5. Closed Mon. & holidays.

Tours
Call (502) 636-2893 for information.

Food & Drink
Café Musée.

J. Paul Getty Museum

17985 Pacific Coast Hwy., Malibu, Calif. 90265
(213) 458-2003

1990 Exhibitions
Thru Jan. 7
Seventeenth-Century Italian Drawings
Includes works by Bernini, Carracci, Reni, Rosa.

Thru Mar. 4
Experimental Photography: The New Subjectivity
The development of photography as an expressive medium, from the 1940s–60s, explored in works by Callahan, Kertész, Siskind, Smith, Sudek.

Jan. 9–Mar. 25
Renaissance and Mannerist Drawings in Northern Europe
Surveys the art of drawing in Germany, Switzerland, and the Low Countries during the 15th and 16th centuries. Includes works by Dürer, Goltzius, Holbein, van Haarlem.

Jan. 16–Apr. 1
The Art of the Written Word: Calligraphy in Medieval and Renaissance Illuminated Manuscripts
Manuscripts from Belgium, England, Germany, Hungary, and Italy from the 9th to 16th centuries.

Mar. 13–May 27
Carleton Watkins Photographs

Mar. 27–June 10
Eighteenth- and Nineteenth-Century Drawings

Memphis, Tenn.

Apr. 17–July 1
The Vision of Tondal: A Masterpiece of Burgundian Illumination

June 12–Aug. 26
Dutch and Flemish Drawings

July 17–Sept. 30
Illuminated Secular Manuscripts

Sept. 11–Nov. 25
Paul Strand: The Portraits

Dec. 4–Feb. 17, 1991
August Sander Photography

Permanent Collection
Extensive holdings of Greek and Roman antiquities; pre 20th-century European paintings, drawings, sculptures, illuminated manuscripts, decorative arts; 19th- and 20th-century American and European photographs. **Highlights:** Greek vases and sculpture; French paneled rooms from the time of Louis XIV to the Napoleonic era; Giambologna, *Bathsheba;* Masaccio, *Saint Andrew;* Raphael, *Christ in Glory;* Terbrugghen, *Bacchante with a Monkey;* photographs by Cameron, Evans, Man Ray, Nadar, Weston. **Architecture:** 1974 re-creation of a first-century Roman country villa with gardens.

Admission
Free; admission by prior reservation; call museum, 9–5. Handicapped accessible.

Hours
Tues.–Sun., 10–5 (entrance closes 4:30). Closed Mon. & holidays.

Tours
Call (213) 458-2003 for information.

Food & Drink
Garden Tea Room: Tues.–Sun., 9:30–4:30.

The Dixon Gallery and Gardens

**4339 Park Ave., Memphis, Tenn. 38117
(901) 761-5250**

1990 Exhibitions
Jan. 14–Feb. 28
Paintings by Daniel Ridgway Knight and Louis Aston Knight: A Father and Son in France

Memphis, Tenn.

Jan. 14–Feb. 28
Three Centuries of Pewter from the Collection of Dr. and Mrs. Justin H. Adler

Mar. 11–Apr. 15
Louis XV and Madame de Pompadour: A Love Affair with Style

Apr.–June
Odilon Redon: The Woodner Collection

Apr. 20–Apr. 22
Flowers and Art: A French Bouquet

July 15–Aug. 26
American Impressionism from the Sheldon Art Gallery

July 15–Sept. 3
Lalique: A Century of Design for a Modern World

Sept. 8–Nov. 10
Illuminations: Images of Landscape in France, 1855–1885

Sept. 9–Nov. 11
Majolica Ware from Southern Collections
About 50 objects illustrate the variety of technical effects and diversity of styles found in Italian majolica.

Nov. 11–Dec. 30
French Military Paintings from the Forbes Collection

Dancer Adjusting her Shoe, 1885, by Edgar Degas. The Dixon Gallery and Gardens.

Permanent Collection
Focuses on French impressionist and postimpressionist painting; 18th- and 19th-century British portraits and landscapes, period furniture, decorative arts. **Highlights:** Cassatt, *The Visitor: Left Profile;* Corot, *Le Paveur de la Route Chailly;* Degas, *Dancer Adjusting Her Shoe;* Renoir, *Le Livre d'Images;* Rodin, *Young Girl with Flowers in Her Hair;* Stout collection of 18th-century German Meissen porcelain. **Architecture:** 1949 Georgian-style complex designed by Staub; 1977 wing; 1986 Georgian-style addition.

Admission
Adults $2; seniors, students, children $1.50; members free. Handicapped accessible.

Hours
Tues.–Sat., 10–5; Sun., 1–5. Closed Mon. & holidays.

Tours
Call (901) 761-5250 for information.

Food & Drink
Terrace Café: Open during selected exhibitions.

Miami, Fla.

Center for the Fine Arts

101 West Flagler St., Miami, Fla. 33130
(305) 375-3000; 375-1700 (recorded)

1990 Exhibitions

Thru Jan. 14
The New Narratology: Examining the Narrative in Image-Text Art

Thru Jan. 14
Vernon Fisher
Features free-standing sculptures, wall pieces, and works on paper, exhibiting Fisher's witty, mordantly literal fusion of language and visual imagery. Catalogue.

Thru Feb. 25
Selected Geometric Abstract Painting in America since 1945
A selection of postwar American paintings including works by Albers, Halley, Kelly, Newman, Reinhardt, Stella.

Mar. 17–May 27
A Golden Age: Art and Society in Hungary (1896–1914)
Presents over 500 paintings, drawings, photographs, posters, ceramics, furniture, textiles, costumes.

June 17–Aug. 19
†*Sounding the Depths: 150 Years of American Seascapes*
Features 80 paintings, photographs, and sculptures, 1820–1986; explores various themes of the individual and the sea.

Nov. 18–Jan. 20, 1991
Hans Hofmann Retrospective
First retrospective since 1966 of the influential teacher and artist who introduced the most avant-garde concepts of European painting to his students in New York beginning in the early 1930s.

Ex Libris–Róbert Kertész, c. 1910, by Attila Sassy. From *A Golden Age: Art and Society in Hungary* at the Center for the Fine Arts, Mar. 17–May 27.

Permanent Collection

No permanent collection. **Architecture:** 1983 building by Johnson.

Admission

Adults $3; groups $2.50; children, 6–12, $2. Handicapped accessible; wheelchairs available.

Hours

Tues.–Sat., 10–5; Thurs., 10–9; Sun., noon–5. Closed Mon.

Tours

Call (305) 375-3000 for information.

Food & Drink

Outdoor café: Tues.–Sat., 11–3. Metrofare snack bars and restaurants: Mon.–Fri., 9–4.

Milwaukee Art Museum

**750 North Lincoln Memorial Dr.,
Milwaukee, Wis. 53202
(414) 271-9508**

1990 Exhibitions
Thru Jan. 7
Currents 16: Terry Winters Drawings
Works by the artist known for his paintings of plants, spores, crystals, and similar types of organic and inorganic forms.

Thru Jan. 14
Renaissance into Baroque: Italian Master Drawings by the Zuccari, 1550–1600
Features 100 of the artists' drawings. Catalogue.

Thru Jan. 21
Frank Stella: The Circuits Prints
Presents the series of mulitmedia large-scale prints made 1981–85; includes trial and progressive proofs.

Thru Jan. 21
Marsden Hartley in Bavaria
Drawings, lithographs, oils, and pastels by the pioneer American modernist during his stay in the alpine village Garmisch-Partenkirchen in the 1930s. Catalogue.

Thru Jan. 28
Gregory Conniff/Frank Gohlke: Two Days in Louisiana
Photographs in black and white by Conniff and in color by Gohlke taken in the Baton Rouge vicinity. Catalogue.

Jan. 25–May 27
Nicholas Nixon: People with Aids
Large-camera black-and-white photographs by Nixon documents the lives of aids victims.

Feb. 2–Mar. 25
10 + 10: Contemporary Soviet and American Painters
Works representing the new avant-garde in the Soviet Union and America.

Feb. 16–May 27
Sumptuous Surrounds: Silver Overlay on Ceramic and Glass
Sophisticated overlay work by prominent art potters and glass blowers of the late 19th and early 20th centuries; includes works by Loetz, Rookwood, Tiffany. Catalogue.

Mar. 15–May 13
Sylvia Sleigh: Invitation to a Voyage and Other Works
Features a panoramic installation, portraits, and nudes by the New York realist painter.

Milwaukee, Wis.

Apr. 6–June 3
Selected Geometric Abstract Painting in America since 1945
A Comprehensive selection of postwar American paintings including works by Albers, Halley, Kelly, Newman, Reinhardt, Stella.

Apr. 7–July 7
Perceptions 1990: Contemporary Wisconsin Art
Features drawings, paintings, handmade paper, and sculptures.

May 25–Aug. 26
Currents 17: Meg Webster
Sculptures using natural materials and an outdoor site-specific sculpture garden by the contemporary Wisconsin artist.

June 7–Sept. 16
Currier & Ives' Best Fifty Revisited
Features the American Historical Print Collectors new selection of the printmakers' best large folios. Catalogue.

June 15–Aug. 26
Word as Image: American Art 1960–1990
Examines the use of language in American art. Catalogue.

July 13–Sept. 9
James Ensor Prints
Prints by the Belgian painter (1860–1949) known as a precursor of expressionism and surrealism, and founder of the Belgian symbolist group Les Vingt.

July 14–Aug. 19
Cross Cultures: Ethnic Themes in Wisconsin Art
Catalogue.

Seated Mythical Animal, 1913, by Franz Marc. Milwaukee Art Museum.

Permanent Collection
Eighteenth- to 20th-century European and American art, decorative art, and photography, including works by German expressionists and American ash can school artists.
Highlights: Archive of the Prairie school of architecture; Bradley collection of early modern and contemporary art; one of the world's largest collections of Haitian art; Fragonard, *Shepherdess;* Johnson, *The Old Stage Coach;* Zurbarán, *Saint Francis.* **Architecture:** 1957 building by Eero Saarinen; 1975 addition by Kahler.

Admission
Adults $3; seniors, students, handicapped $1.50; children under 12, free, Milwaukee County residents, Wed. & Sat. 10–noon, free. Handicapped accessible.

Hours
Tues.–Wed. & Fri.–Sat., 10–5; Thurs., noon–9; Sun., noon–5. Closed Mon., Jan. 1, Dec. 25.

Tours
Call (414) 271-9508 for information.

Food & Drink
Museum Buffet: Open during museum hours.

The Minneapolis Institute of Arts

2400 Third Ave. South, Minneapolis, Minn. 55404
(612) 870-3046

1990 Exhibitions
Thru Jan. 7
Inside Outside: Bookbindings and Endpapers
Seventeenth- to 20th-century examples from the institute's permanent collection.

Thru Jan. 7
The Photographs of Lee Miller
The first retrospective since 1932 of the work of this noted photographer and war correspondent. Catalogue.

Thru Feb. 11
†*Jim Dine Drawings*
First comprehensive exhibition of the master draftsman's recent drawings. Catalogue.

Jan. 28–Mar. 25
†*Impressionism: Selected Paintings from Five Museums*
Features 85 paintings and sculptures by the celebrated impressionists and postimpressionists Bonnard, Cassatt, Degas, van Gogh, Manet, Monet, Pissarro, Renoir.

Jan. 20–Mar. 25
Minor White
Retrospective of 100 the noted photographer's career.

Mar. 4–June
Whistler's Chelsea
Prints and books by Rossetti, Sargeant, Swinburne, Wilde, and others.

May 5–Aug. 12
*In Our Time: The World as Seen by Magnum Photographers

Permanent Collection
African and Asian art; European and American paintings, prints, drawings, sculptures, photographs, decorative art; period rooms; American textiles. **Highlights:** Chinese bronzes, jades, silks; Greco-Roman Doryphoros; American and British silver; works by Magritte, Poussin, Rembrandt,

Minneapolis, Minn.

Tintoretto. **Architecture:** 1914 building by McKim, Mead, and White; 1974 wing by Tange, URTEC, and Parker Klein Associates.

Admission
Fee. Entrance fee for selected exhibitions.
Handicapped accessible.

Hours
Tues.–Sat., 10–5; Thurs., 10–9; Sun., noon–5. Closed Mon., July 4, Thanksgiving, Dec. 25.

Tours
Tues.–Sun. at 2; Thurs. at 7; Sat.–Sun. at 1. American Sign Language interpretation first Sun. of month; call (612) 870-3046 for information.

Food & Drink
Studio Restaurant: Tues.–Sun., 11:30–3. Friends Coffee Shop: Open during museum hours.

Walker Art Center

Vineland Place, Minneapolis, Minn. 55403
(612) 375-7622; 375-7636 (recorded)

Without Words, 1988, by Judith Shea. Minneapolis Sculpture Garden at the Walker Art Center.

1990 Exhibitions
Indefinite
Cowles Conservatory
A three-part glass house containing horticultural installation, and the sculpture *Standing Glass Fish* by Gehry.

Thru Jan. 21
Graphic Design in America: A Visual Language History
Explores the aesthetic and social evolution of graphic design with works by Bass, Bayer, Chermayeff, Wurman, and others. Catalogue.

Thru Feb. 11
Architecture Tomorrow: Tod Williams, Billie Tsien
Third exhibition of a series; features the experimental work of two noted New York architects.

Feb. 18–May 13
Jasper Johns: Printed Symbols
Retrospective of the career of a major American artist—from *Target*, his first black-and-white lithograph (1960), to multicolored etchings (1987). Catalogue.

June 10–Sept. 2
The Photography of Invention: American Pictures of the Eighties
Celebrates photography's 150th anniversary with 160 works by 80 American photographers. Catalogue.

Mountainville, N.Y.

June 17–Aug. 26
Architecture Tomorrow: Stanley Saitowitz
Features the work of the San Franciscan architect.

Oct. 7–Dec. 30
Art into Life: Russian Constructivism 1914–1932

Permanent Collection
Primarily 20th-century art of all major movements; 7.5-acre outdoor sculpture garden containing works by acknowledged modernists and leading contemporaries. **Highlights:** Hockney, *Hollywood Hills House;* Hopper, *Office at Night;* Johns, complete collection of 242 prints; Kelly, *Double Curve;* Kiefer, *Die Ordnung der Engel;* Marc, *The Large Blue Horses;* Moore, *Reclining Mother and Child;* Noguchi, *Judith;* O'Keeffe, *Lake George Barns;* Minneapolis Sculpture Garden: forty works by established 20th-century masters and by leading contemporaries. **Architecture:** 1971 building, 1983 addition and 1988 Minneapolis Sculpture Garden by Barnes.

Admission
Adults $3; students, children, 12–18, & groups of 10 or more, $2 per person; seniors, members, children under 12; Thurs., free. Handicapped accessible.

Hours
Tues.–Sat., 10–8 (selected exhibitions 5–8); Sun., 11–5. Closed Mon. & major holidays.

Tours
Thurs. at 11; Sat.–Sun. at 2. For group tour reservations call (612) 375-7611.

Food & Drink
Gallery 8 Restaurant: Tues.–Sun., 11:30–3.

Storm King Art Center

**Old Pleasant Hill Rd., Mountainville, N.Y.   10953
(914) 534-3115**

1990 Exhibitions
Indefinite
Alexander Calder: Five Grand Stabiles
Large-scale outdoor sculptures made late in the career of the imaginative American artist; first U.S. presentation.

May 21–Oct. 31
Alice Aycock: Sculpture and Drawings
Features 15 outsized drawings and fanciful sculptures using wood, machine parts, mirrors, brass, and other innovative materials. Catalogue.

New Haven, Conn.

Permanent Collection
Sculpture park and museum with more than 100 objects including work by Calder, Caro, Hepworth, Moore, Nevelson, Smith, Snelson, di Suvero. **Highlights:** Work by Caro, Newman, Smith. **Architecture:** 1934–35 French Norman-style building.

Admission
Adults $5; seniors & students $3; members & children under 5 free. Handicapped accessible.

Hours
Apr. 1–Nov. 30, daily, noon–5:30. Closed Dec. 1–Mar. 31.

Tours
For group tour reservations call (914) 534-3190.

Food & Drink
Extensively landscaped picnic area.

Mr. and Mrs. John Gravenor and their Daughters, Elizabeth and Ann, c. 1750, by Thomas Gainsborough. Yale Center for British Art.

Yale Center for British Art
**1080 Chapel St., New Haven, Conn. 06520
(203) 432-2850**

1990 Exhibitions
Thru Jan. 14
Coracle Press
Graphics produced by the noted press, 1975–87; including invitations, artists' books, monographs. Catalogue.

Thru. Jan. 28
Frederick H. Evans: "The Desired Haven"
Features photographs that capture the solemn beauty of the great English cathedrals.

Feb. 6–Apr. 1
John Copley (1875–1950)
Presents graphic works that bridge pre- and postwar schools of figurative art. Catalogue.

Feb. 21–Apr. 29
Pleasures and Pastimes
Toys, games, and children's books as well as views of indoor and outdoor sporting events, festive occasions, theatrical events, seasonal recreations, and everyday diversions enjoyed by 18th-and 19th-century Britains are featured.

Apr. 20–June 24
Snuff Boxes, 1700–1880

May 23–July 15
Twentieth-Century Acquisitions: Works on Paper
Works representing trends in contemporary British art.

New Haven, Conn.

Permanent Collection
Focuses on British art, life, and thought beginning with the Elizabethan period; emphasis on work created between the birth of Hogarth in 1697 and the death of Turner in 1851, considered the golden age of English art. **Highlights:** Constable, *Hadleigh Castle;* Gainsborough, *The Gravenor Family;* Reynolds, *Mrs. Abington as Miss Prue in Congreve's "Love for Love"*; Rubens, *Peace Embracing Plenty;* Stubbs, *A Lion Attacking a Horse;* Turner, *Dort or Dordrecht: The Dort Packet-Boat from Rotterdam Becalmed.* **Architecture:** 1977 building by Kahn.

Admission
Free. Handicapped accessible.

Hours
Tues.–Sat., 10–5; Sun., 2–5. Closed Mon., Jan. 1, July 4, Thanksgiving, Dec. 24–25 & 31.

Tours
Call (203) 432-2858.

Yale University Art Gallery

**1111 Chapel at York St., New Haven, Conn. 06520
(203) 432-0600**

1990 Exhibitions
Thru Jan. 3
American Daguerreotypes from the Matthew R. Isenburg Collection

Jan. 15–Mar. 3
Paul Outerbridge a Singular Aesthetic: Photographs and Drawings, 1921–1941
Features 50 rarely exhibited black-and-white and color images reflecting the influence of the world wars and European surrealism. Catalogue.

Jan. 27–Mar. 11
The Art Museums of Louis I. Kahn
First in-depth analysis of the architect's projects, featuring 120 drawings and five models. Catalogue.

Rooms by the Sea, 1951, by Edward Hopper. Yale University Art Gallery.

Apr. 4–June 10
Childe Hassam: An Island Garden Revisited
First major exhibition to focus solely on the artist's impressionist paintings of the Isles of Shoals. Includes oils, watercolors, pastels. Catalogue.

Apr. 19–June 3
Kiyochika: Artist of Meiji Japan
Includes landscapes (1876–88), still lifes, prints, political cartoons (1880s), war triptychs, and woodblock illustrations of Japan's war with China (1884).

New Orleans, La.

July 1–Aug. 30
Selected Geometric Abstract Painting in America since 1945

Permanent Collection
Ranges from ancient Egyptian dynasties to the present: Asian art, including Japanese screens, ceramics, prints; artifacts from ancient Dura-Europos; Italian Renaissance art; 19th- and 20th-century European paintings; early modern works by Kandinsky, Léger, Picasso; American art through the 20th century, featuring paintings, sculptures, furniture, silver, pewter. **Highlights:** Reconstructed Mithraic shrine; van Gogh, *The Night Café;* Malevich, *The Knife Grinder;* Smibert, *The Bermuda Group;* Trumbull, *The Declaration of Independence;* sculpture by Moore, Nevelson, Smith. **Architecture:** 1928 Italianate building by Swartwout; 1953 building by Kahn.

Admission
Free. Handicapped accessible.

Hours
Tues.–Sat., 10–5; Sun., 2–5; mid-Sept.–mid-May, Thurs., 10–8. Closed Mon., Jan. 1, July 4, Thanksgiving, Dec. 24–25 & 31.

Tours
Call (203) 432-0620 for information.

New Orleans Museum of Art

P.O. Box 19123
City Park, New Orleans, La. 70179
(504) 488-2631

1990 Exhibitions
Thru Jan. 7
All Aboard: Children's Favorites
Antique trains amid a miniature panoramic landscape.

Thru Jan. 7
Cecil Beaton Retrospective
Examines the British designer and photographer's influence on 20th-century style and consciousness through his costumes, films, interior decorations, paintings, and photographs, including his work for *My Fair Lady.*

Jan. 27–June 24
The Passion of Rodin: Sculpture from the B. Gerald Cantor Collections
Surveys the range of Rodin's work with 60 of the master French artist's sculptures from the world's largest private Rodin collection.

Feb. 2–Mar. 11
Black History Month Exhibition

1990 Color Portfolio

Little May Day Procession, by William Glackens. From *American Paintings from the Manoogian Collection.*

Birds of the Bagaduce, 1939, by Marsden Hartley. From *Sounding the Depths: 150 Years of American Seascape.* Courtesy AFA.

Seated Peasant, 1895–1900, by Paul Cézanne. From *The Annenberg Collection: Masterpieces of Impressionism and Postimpressionism.*

Houses in the Courtyard, 1895–96, by Pierre Bonnard. From *Pierre Bonnard: The Graphic Art.*

The Moroccans, 1916, by Henri Matisse. Museum of Modern Art, N.Y.

Orange Sweater, 1955, by Elmer Bischoff. From *Bay Area Figurative Art.*

Mirabilia Mundi, 13th c., by Hugo of Fouilloy. The J. Paul Getty Museum.

Travel Postcard (Pozdrav z cesty), 1923, by Karel Teige. From *Czech Modernism: 1900–1945.*

Gables I, Lunenburg, 1925, by Lyonel Feininger. Smith College Museum of Art.

The West Wind, 1917, by Tom Thomson. Art Gallery of Ontario.

The White Bridge, after 1895, by John Twachtman. From *John Twachtman: Connecticut Landscapes.*

Carolina Shout, 1974, by Romare Bearden. The Mint Museum of Art.

Spoonbridge and Cherry, 1987–1988, by Claes Oldenburg and Coosje van Bruggen. Minneapolis Sculpture Garden, Walker Art Center.

The Church of St. Ludwig in Munich, 1908, by Wassily Kandinsky. From *Expressionism and Modern German Painting from the Thyssen-Bornemisza Collection.*

Untitled, 1983, by Keith Haring. Jacksonville Art Museum.

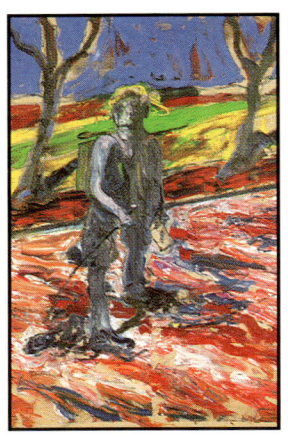

Study for Portrait of Van Gogh III, 1957, by Francis Bacon. From *Francis Bacon Retrospective*.

Necklaces and Disc-shaped Cast Gold Beads, Ghana. From *Gold of Africa: Jewelry and Ornaments from Ghana, Côte d'Ivoire, Mali and Senegal*. Courtesy AFA.

Synchromy in Orange: To Form, 1913–14, by Morgan Russell. Albright-Knox Art Gallery.

Red Dancers on the Western Shore, 1986, by Jim Dine. From *Jim Dine Drawngs*.

Bilderlager, 1988, by Thomas Huber. Museum of Fine Arts, Boston. From *German Art of the Late Eighties*.

La Pia De'Tolomei, 1880, by Dante Gabriel Rossetti. Spencer Museum of Art.

Portrait of the Artist's Wife, Jeanne Hebuterne, by Amedeo Modigliani. Norton Simon Art Foundation.

"Peacock" Window, c. 1912, by Louis Comfort Tiffany. From *The Masterworks of Louis Comfort Tiffany*.

The Olive Grove, by Vincent Van Gogh. From *Impressionism: Selections from Five American Museums*.

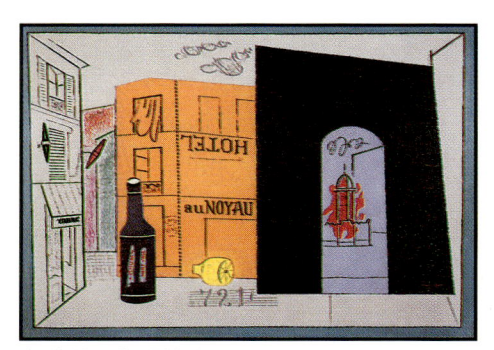

Arch Hotel, 1929, by Stuart Davis. Sheldon Memorial Art Gallery. From *Of Time and the City: American Modernism from the Sheldon Memorial Art Gallery*. Courtesy AFA.

Piccola Russa, 1913, by Mario Cavaglieri. From *Gardens and Ghettos: The Art of Jewish Life in Italy*.

Portrait of Shah Jahan, Page from the Late Shah Jahan Album, c. 1635, Mogul. From *Romance of the Taj Mahal*.

Tarquin and Lucretia, by Titian. High Museum of Art.

The Rainbow, 1913, by Robert Delaunay. Honolulu Academy of Arts.

Le Beau Temps, 1939, by Man Ray. On loan to Philadelphia Museum of Art.

The Red Maple, by A. Y. Jackson. National Gallery of Canada.

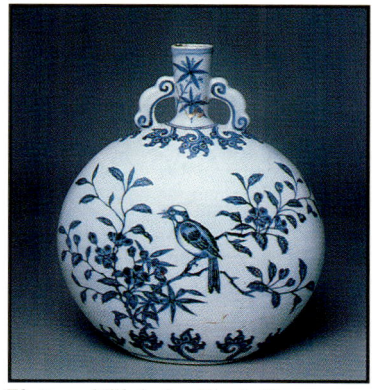

Flattened Globular Flask (Bao yue ping, Precious Moon Vase), Jingdezhen porcelain. From *Imperial Taste: Chinese Ceramics from the Percival David Foundation.*

Buddha's Court, 1964, by Helen Frankenthaler. From *Helen Frankenthaler: A Paintings Retrospective.*

The Newspaper, by Edouard Vuillard. From *The Intimate Interiors of Edouard Vuillard.*

Young Woman Sewing, 1923, by Gari Melchers. From *Gari Melchers: A Retrospective.*

Flag of Mother and Seven Children, Fante Group, Ghana. From *Icons: Ideals and Power in the Art of Africa.*

Early Morning After a Storm at Sea, 1902, by Winslow Homer. The Cleveland Museum of Art.

Self Portrait with Rita, 1922, by Thomas Hart Benton. From *Thomas Hart Benton: An American Original.*

Kneeling Woman, 100 B.C.–300 A.D., Mexico. From *Little People of the Earth* at Denver Art Museum June 23–Sept. 9.

On the Cache, La Poudre River, Colorado, by Worthington Whittredge. From *Worthington Whittredge.*

A La Cremerie, 1910, by Martha Walter. Terra Museum of American Art.

Feb. 9–Apr. 1
Robert Warrens Retrospective
Examines the remarkable narrative syle of the contemporary Louisiana artist.

Apr. 21–June 10
Robert Willson: Glass Sculpture
Exquisite creations by the artist credited with innovating the history of glassmaking.

May 5–July 1
Awards in the Visual Arts IX

June 23–Aug. 12
George Ohr: The Mad Potter of Biloxi
Features eccentric pottery of compelling modernity, with twisted and crumpled forms, bold colors, and a distinctive blending of humor and art. Catalogue.

Aug. 4–Oct. 14
Diverse Images II: Photography at NOMA
Surveys the history of photography with 175 images from the museum's permanent collection.

Sept. 8–Oct. 14
Julio Sequeira: Images of Eden

Nov. 9–Dec. 30
Down River: Currents of Style in Louisiana Painting, 1800–1950
Documents the art styled that emerged at particular periods in the history of Louisiana art.

Berenice Abbott in Veil and Ruff Posed before Man Ray, Composition, 1922, by Man Ray. New Orleans Museum of Art.

Permanent Collection
Kress collection of Renaissance and baroque painting; French art with paintings by Degas, who visited New Orleans in 1871–72; art of the Americas surveys the cultural heritage of North, Central, and South America. **Highlights:** Degas gallery, especially *Portrait of Estelle Muson Degas;* Federal- and Louisiana-style period rooms containing 18th- and 19th-century furniture and decorative arts; Fabergé Easter eggs from the Russian imperial collection and the jeweled Basket of Lilies of the Valley created for Empress Alexandra; Vigée-Lebrun, *Marie Antoinette, Queen of France.* **Architecture:** 1911 beaux-arts structure by Marx in a 1,500-acre city park.

Admission
Adults $4; seniors & children under 18 $2. Thurs., free for Louisiana residents. Entrance fee for selected exhibitions.

Hours
Tues.–Sun., 10–5. Closed Mon. & holidays.

Tours
Call (504) 488-2631 for information.

New York, N.Y.

Cooper-Hewitt Museum

**The Smithsonian's National Museum of Design
2 East 91st St., New York, N.Y. 10128
(212) 860-6868**

1990 Exhibitions
Thru Jan. 7
Jewelry: Selections from the Cooper-Hewitt Museum Collection
Over 100 examples of the jeweler's art from 19th-century England, Italy, France, America, and the Near and Far East.

Thru Feb. 18
McKnight Kauffer: Graphic Art and Theater Design
Presents work by the American-born graphic and theater designer, noted for his British Rail and American Airline posters and stage and costume designs for de Valois's ballet *Checkmate*, first staged in 1937.

Thru Mar. 11
The Intimate World of Alexander Calder
Over 300 informal works—kitchen accouterments, toys, jewelry, caricatures—made by the designer and sculptor as presents or whimsies for his family and friends.

Apr. 1–Sept.
Color, Surface, Light: Contemporary Textiles
Includes unique works produced world-wide.

May 22–Oct. 14
The Doghouse
An exhibition specifically designed for the blind and visually impaired. Presents doghouse designs in the museum's garden and a group of drawings in a nearby gallery.

Permanent Collection
Covers 3,000 years of design history in cultures around the world. Major holdings include drawings, prints, textiles, furniture, metalwork, ceramics, glass, woodwork, wall coverings. **Highlights:** Egyptian, Islamic, Mediterranean, and Near Eastern textiles from the third to the 15th century; large group of Homer drawings; 19th-century jewelry by Castellani and Giuliano; glass desk by Bourgeois; chromium steel and canvas chair by Breuer. **Architecture:** 1901 Carnegie mansion by Babb, Cook, and Willard.

Admission
Adults $3; seniors & students under 12 $1.50. Tues., 5–9, free. Handicapped accessible.

Hours
Tues., 10–9; Wed.–Sat., 10–5; Sun., noon–5. Closed Mon., Jan. 1, Thanksgiving, Dec. 25.

Tours
Call (212) 860-6871.

Winter Sales Are Best Reached by Underground, 1924, by E. McKnight Kauffer. From *Edward McKnight Kauffer: Graphic Art and Theater Design* at the Cooper-Hewitt Museum, thru Feb. 18.

The Frick Collection

1 East 70th St., New York, N.Y. 10021
(212) 288-0700

1990 Exhibitions
Thru Jan. 14
In Pursuit of Quality/The Kimbell Art Museum: Twenty-five Years of Collecting Old Masters

Feb. 5–Apr. 8
Rowlandson: Drawings and Watercolors
Features 80 works by the popular Georgian period English artist renowned as an acerbic social commentator. Includes hunting, boxing, racing, and courting scenes as well as landscapes and portraits. Catalogue.

June 25–Aug. 19
Seventeenth-Century Chinese Porcelain from the Collection of Sir Michael Butler
Catalogue.

Sept. 19–Nov. 18
The Drawings of Adolph Menzel
About 100 works by the German artist (1815–1905) considered by many the greatest naturalist since Dürer. Catalogue.

Permanent Collection
Includes works by Goya, Ingres, Rembrandt, Renoir, Titian, Van Dyck; Renaissance sculptures; Renaissance and French 18th-century furniture; Sèvres porcelains; Limoges enamels. Highlights: Bellini, *Saint Francis in the Desert;* della Francesca, *Saint John the Evangelist;* van Eyck, *Virgin with Child, with Saints and Donor;* Holbein, *Sir Thomas More* and *Thomas Cromwell;* Rembrandt, *Self-Portrait*; Stuart, *George Washington*. **Architecture:** 1931–41 Frick mansion by Hastings; 1977 extension and garden.

Admission
Adults $3; seniors & students $1.50; children under 16 must be accompanied by adult; children under 10 not admitted. Handicapped accessible; wheelchairs available, call for reservation.

Hours
Tues.–Sat., 10–6; Sun., 1–6; Feb. 12, Election Day, Nov. 11, 1–6. Closed Mon., Jan. 1, July 4, Thanksgiving, Dec. 24–25.

Tours
Call (212) 288-0700 for information.

Lady Hamilton as "Nature," 1782, by George Romney. The Frick Collection.

New York, N.Y.

The Jewish Museum

**1109 Fifth Ave. at 92nd St., New York, N.Y. 10128
(212) 860-1889; 860-1888 (recorded)**

1990 Exhibitions
Thru Feb. 1
†*Gardens and Ghettos: The Art of Jewish Life in Italy*
More than 340 works, from ancient Roman architectural fragments, gold, glass, illuminated Renaissance manuscripts, baroque textiles and silver to 19th- and 20th-century works by Levi, Modigliani, and others. Catalogue.

Thru Dec.
Exodus and Exile: Two Thousand Years in Ancient Israel
Over 200 archaic objects of ritual, historical, and domestic significance from ancient Israel and surrounding countries.

Mar.–May
Between the Wars: Art and Resistance in Düsseldorf
Displays the work of 45 artists, depicting their responses to the political situation during the Weimar and Nazi periods.

Spring–Summer
Jews of the Ottoman Empire
Explores the material culture of the Sephardic communities of the western Ottoman Empire and their transition into modernity. Includes festive costumes, colorful textiles, ceremonial objects.

Permanent Collection
Dedicated to preserving and interpreting 4,000 years of Jewish culture. Paintings, graphics, and sculptures inspired by the Jewish experience; archaeological artifacts; objects from Central European homes and synagogues brought to the museum after the Holocaust; Israeli art; National Jewish Archive of Broadcasting. **Highlights:** Ancient Israeli ossuary; Rembrandt, *The Triumph of Mordecai;* paintings by Chagall and Epstein. **Architecture:** 1908 Warburg mansion by Gilbert; 1959 sculpture court; 1963 List Building.

Admission
Adults $4.50; seniors, students, children, 6–16, $2.50. Tues., 5–8, free. Handicapped accessible.

Hours
Sun., 11–6; Mon.–Thurs., noon–5; Tues., noon–8. Closed Fri.–Sat., major Jewish holidays, national holidays.

Tours
Call (212) 860-1863.

Sogni (Dreams), 1896, by Vittorio Corcos. From *Gardens and Ghettos: The Art of Jewish Life in Italy* at The Jewish Museum, thru Feb. 1.

Metropolitan Museum of Art

**Fifth Ave. at 82d St., New York, N.Y. 10028
(212) 879-5500; 535-7710 (recorded)**

1990 Exhibitions

Thru Jan. 5
The Crane Pacific Expedition, 1928–1929: The Sepik River Photographs
Rare black-and-white images taken by members of a privately sponsored expedition to New Guinea.

Thru Jan. 7
Velázquez
First comprehensive display of the artist's greatest paintings; includes nearly 40 works, most from the Prado, many never seen outside Spain.

Thru Jan. 7
Manifestations of Kannon
Japanese Buddhist painting and sculpture.

Thru Jan. 14
American Pastels in the Metropolitan Museum of Art: 1880–1930
Presents 40 works by 22 artists including Cassatt, Dove, O'Keeffe, Whistler.

Thru. Jan. 21
Canaletto
Surveys the artist's career as a painter and draftsman, emphasizing his early works; includes about 125 paintings and drawings by the Venetian view painter.

Thru Jan. 21
Views of Venice
Features about 30 Canaletto prints and 40 paintings, drawings, prints, and printed books by Bellotto, Carlevaris, Marieschi, and others.

Thru Feb. 4
†Pierre Bonnard: The Graphic Works
Celebrates the artist's vision of everyday life; includes prints, drawings, illustrated books, oil paintings. Catalogue.

Thru Feb. 4
A Selection of Prints from the Bequest of Scofield Thayer
Presents more than 50 lithographs and etchings from Toulouse-Lautrec to Matisse.

Thru Feb. 25
†American Paintings from the Manoogian Collection
Nineteenth-century works by Bierstadt, Bingham, Cropsey, Eakins, Heade. Catalogue.

New York, N.Y.

Thru Mar. 11
†*Gold of Africa: Jewelry and Ornaments from Ghana, Côte d'Ivoire, Mali, and Senegal*
Jewelry and royal regalia primarily made by the Akan-speaking peoples in the 19th and 20th centuries. Catalogue.

Thru Apr. 1
Twentieth-Century Masters: The Jacques and Natasha Gelman Collection
Presents paintings, works on paper, and sculptures; includes works by Braque, Matisse, Miró, Picasso. Catalogue.

Thru Apr. 15
The Age of Napoleon: Costume from Revolution to Empire
Displays 120 examples of French dress, costumes, military uniforms, and textiles; includes paintings, jewelry, and decorative art objects.

Thru May 13
Master Drawings from the Woodner Collection
About 150 works represent periods and styles from the early Renaissance to the 20th century; includes works by Cellini, Cézanne, Durer, Goya, Raphael, Redon, Rembrandt, Seurat, Watteau. Catalogue.

Thru July 29
Japanese Art from the Gerry Collection
Includes Japanese ceramics and Buddhist art and Muromachi period screens. Catalogue.

May 2–Nov. 4
Art of Central Africa: Masterpieces from the Berlin Museum Für Völkerkunde
Features about 60 sculptures from the area. Catalogue.

May 23–July 29
Poussin to Matisse
An exchange exhibition with the USSR's Hermitage and Pushkin museums; includes works by Bonnard, Boucher, Cézanne, Gauguin, Lorrain, Matisse, Poussin, Renoir.

Early June–Sept.
A Selection of Chinese Ceramics from the Adele and Stanley Herzman Collection
Exhibits about 90 works, ranging from the Han dynasty (206 B.C.–A.D. 220) through the Qing dynasty (1644–1912).

Permanent Collection
One of the largest and most comprehensive museums in the world, covering in depth every culture and period. **Highlights:** Babylonian Striding Lions; Temple of Dendur; grand drawing room in American wing; Astor Court Chinese rock garden; Song dynasty Tribute Horses; Cantor Roof Garden sculpture (May 1–Oct. 30); Brown collection of musical instruments; Louis XIV bedroom; Bingham, *Fur Traders Descending the Missouri;* Brueghel, *The Harvesters;* Church, *Heart of the Andes;* Degas, *Dance Class;* van Eyck,

Crucifixion; El Greco, *View of Toledo;* Leutze, *Washington Crossing the Delaware;* Matisse, *Nasturtiums and "Dance";* Picasso, *Gertrude Stein;* Rembrandt, *Aristotle Contemplating the Bust of Homer;* Velázquez, *Juan de Pareja;* Vermeer, *Young Woman with a Water Jug.* **Architecture:** 1880 building by Vaux and Mould; 1902 central pavilion by Hunt; 1913 wings by McKim, Mead, and White; 1975 Lehman Wing; 1979 Sackler Wing, 1980 American Wing, 1982 Rockefeller Wing by Roche, Dinkeloo, and Associates; 1987 Lila Acheson Wallace Wing for 20th-century art.

Admission
Donation suggested: Adults $5; seniors & children $2.50; children under 12 accompanied by adult free. Entrance fee for selected exhibitions. Handicapped accessible.

Hours
Tues.–Thurs. & Sun., 9:30–5:15; Fri.–Sat., 9:30–8:45. Closed Mon., Jan. 1, Thanksgiving, Dec. 25.

Tours
Daily: Call museum for information.

Food & Drink
Cafeteria: Tues.–Thur. & Sun., 9:30–10:30 (continental breakfast), 11–4:30; Fri.–Sat., 9:30–10:30 (continental breakfast), 11–4:30, 5–8. Restaurant: Tues.–Thurs. & Sun., 11:30–3:30; Fri.–Sat., 11:30–8; for reservations call (212) 570-3964. Bar: Tues.–Thurs. & Sun., 11:30–4:30; Fri.–Sat., 11:30–8. Dining Room: Brunch only Sat.–Sun., 11:30–2:30, for reservations call (212) 879-5500, ext. 3614.

Metropolitan Branches

The Cloisters
Fort Tryon Park, New York, N.Y. 10040
(212) 923-3700

Terrace at Sainte-Adresse, by Claude Monet. The Metropolitan Museum of Art

The Museum of Modern Art

11 West 53d St., New York, N.Y. 10019
(212) 708-9400

1990 Exhibitions
Thru Jan. 2
Projects: Houston Conwill
An installation entitled *Chapel of Justice* by the New York-based artist mixes religious and secular imagery to underscore the continual challenges facing the American judicial system.

Thru Jan. 9
Kayserzinn Pewter
Unusual pewter by sculptor Leven of the German firm J. P. Kayser and Sohn.

New York, N.Y.

Thru Jan. 9
New Photography 5
Introduces emerging photographers. Includes images by Massachusetts artist Vincent Borrelli, West German Thomas Florschuetz, and Californian Mike Mandel.

Thru Jan. 16
Picasso and Braque: Pioneering Cubism
Explores the development of cubism by leaders of the movement; includes paintings, collages, construction sculptures, drawings. Catalogue.

Thru Mar. 13
For Twenty Years: Editions Schellmann
Celebrates the anniversary of the innovative Munich-based publisher with works by more than 20 artists illustrating Schellmann's pioneering vision.

Feb. 10–Apr. 24
Robert Moskowitz
Retrospective of the contemporary American artist who gained recognition with the "new image" painters of the 1970s.

Feb. 18–May 29
Photography until Now
Celebrates the anniversary of the medium with over 250 images, focusing on the relationship of pictorial form and evolution of the photographic craft. Catalogue.

May 24–Aug. 28
†*Francis Bacon*
Surveys the achievement of the contemporary British painter, from his daring figure studies of the 1940s to very recent, vigorously inventive works. Catalogue.

June 21–Sept. 4
Architectural Drawings of the Russian Avant-garde, 1917–1935
Dramatic avant-garde drawings and models by Russian constructivist architects Ginsburg, Leonidov, Melnikov, Moisei, the Vesnin brothers, and others. Catalogue.

June 21–Sept. 4
Matisse in Morocco
Features the artist's work from his two Moroccan visits of 1912–13; includes paintings and drawings from the USSR's Pushkin and Hermitage museums as well as other public and private collections. Catalogue.

Oct. 7–Jan. 15, 1991
High and Low: Modern Art and Popular Culture
Includes work by Dubuffet, Duchamp, Guston, Lichtenstein, Oldenburg, Picasso, Warhol. Catalogue.

Permanent Collection
Masterpieces of modern art by nearly every major artist of

this century: Paintings, sculptures, prints, drawings, illustrated books, architectural designs, photographs, films.
Highlights: Boccioni, *The City Rises;* Cézanne, *The Bather;* Chagall, *I and the Village;* van Gogh, *Portrait of Joseph Roulin* and *Starry Night;* Hopper, *House by the Railroad;* Matisse, *The Blue Window* and nine-panel *The Swimming Pool;* Mondrian, *Broadway Boogie-Woogie;* Monet, *Poplars at Giverny* and *Water Lilies;* Picasso, *Demoiselles d'Avignon* and *Three Musicians;* Rauschenberg, *Bed;* Rousseau, *The Sleeping Gypsy;* sculpture garden. **Architecture:** 1939 building by Goodwin and Stone; 1984 expansion and renovation by Pelli and Gruen.

Admission
Adults $6; seniors $3; students with ID $3.50; members & children under 16 accompanied by adult, free. Thurs., 5–9, donation suggested. Handicapped accessible; wheelchairs available.

Hours
Thurs., 11–9; Fri.–Tues., 11–6. Closed Wed. & Dec. 25.

Tours
Mon.–Fri. at 12:30 & 3; Thurs. at 5:30 & 7.

Food & Drink
Garden Café: Thurs., 11–8; Fri.–Tues., 11–4:30.

The New Museum of Contemporary Art

583 Broadway, New York, N.Y. 10012
(212) 219-1355 (recorded)

1990 Exhibitions
Thru Feb. 4
Annette Lemieux: Appearance of Sound
Six multimedia canvases use photographically derived images to suggest the rhythms and patterns of sound.

Thru Feb. 4
Australian Videos
Features documentary and narrative works.

Thru Feb. 4
Eat Me/Drink Me/Love Me: Installation by Martha Fleming and Lynne Lapointe
Site-specific multimedia installation inspired by "The Goblin Market," a fantastic tale of feminine temptation and redemption by 19th-century English poet Christina Rossetti.

Feb. 15–Apr. 8
Mary Kelly's Interim
Explores the representations of women and aging.

New York, N.Y.

Feb. 15–Apr. 8
Reggie's Third World of Soul: Installation by Reginald Hudlin
Features a satirical video-sculpture shown on monitors marked *Black, White, Mixed Couples.*

May 10–July 15
The Decade Show
Multicultural, multidisciplinary views of the 1980s in a variety of mediums by over 90 artists.

Permanent Collection
To maintain a constant focus on recent works the permanent collection consists of works retained for a ten-year period: paintings, sculptures, prints, drawings, photographs, videotapes. **Architecture:** 1896 Astor building by Cleverdon and Putzel.

Admission
Donation suggested: Adults $3.50; seniors, artists, students $2.50; children under 12 free.

Hours
Wed.–Thurs. & Sun., noon–6; Fri.–Sat., noon–8. Closed Mon.–Tues. & some holidays, call for information.

Tours
Call for information.

The Solomon R. Guggenheim Museum

**1071 Fifth Ave., New York, N.Y. 10128
(212) 360-3500**

1990 Exhibitions
Thru Feb. 11
Jenny Holzer
Texts ranging from aphorisms to lengthier meditations about modern life and the human condition. Catalogue.

The museum will be closed from spring 1990 to fall 1991 for complete renovation of the original building.

Permanent Collection
Nineteenth- and 20th-century works including contemporary and avant-garde paintings; paintings by Appel, Bacon, Bonnard, Cézanne, Chagall, Davis, Dubuffet, Gris, Kokoschka, Louis, Marc, Miró, Modigliani, Mondrian, Pollock, Rousseau, Seurat, Soulages, Villon; sculptures by Archipenko, Arp, Brancusi, Pevsner, Smith. **Highlights:** Cézanne, *Man with Crossed Arms;* Gris, *Still Life;* comprehensive collection of works by Kandinsky and Klee; Louis,

New York, N.Y.

Saraband; Mondrian, *Composition;* Picasso, *Mandolin and Guitar;* Pissarro, *The Hermitage at Pontoise.* **Architecture:** 1959 building by Wright; early 1990s wing by Gwathmey & Siegel Associates under construction.

Admission
Adults $4.50; seniors & students with ID $2.50; children under 7 free. Tues., 5–7:45, free. Handicapped accessible; wheelchairs available.

Hours
Tues., 11–7:45; Wed.–Sun., 11–4:45. Closed Mon. & holidays, call for information.

Tours
Call (212) 360-3558.

Whitney Museum of American Art

945 Madison Ave., New York, N.Y. 10021
(212) 570-3600; 570-3676 (branch information)

1990 Exhibitions
Indefinite
Twentieth-Century American Art: Highlights of the Permanent Collection III and the Calder Circus

Thru Feb. 11
†*Thomas Hart Benton: An American Original*
Colorful and explosively energetic murals and easel paintings are featured in the first major retrospective of this famous American regionalist; held on the centennial of his birth. Catalogue.

Thru Feb. 18
Image World: Art and Media Culture
Examines how artists have responded to media culture; includes more than 100 works in a variety of media by Acconci, Burden, Koons, Kruger, Prince, Rauschenberg, Rosenquist, Warhol.

Mar. 2–May 20
Post Minimalism: American Sculpture, 1965–1975
Explores work by leading American sculptors.

May 31–Sept. 2
†*The Art of Maurice Brazil Prendergast*
A historic retrospective of the career of Prendergast, whose watercolor and oil paintings considerably influenced the development of early 20th-century American art.

Three Flags, 1958, by Jasper Johns. Whitney Museum of American Art.

New York, N.Y.

June 21–Sept. 17
Hans Hofmann
First retrospective since 1966 of the influential teacher and artist who introduced the most avant-garde concepts of European painting to his students in New York beginning in the early 1930s.

Sept. 14–Nov. 26
Burgoyne Diller

Permanent Collection
Comprehensive holdings of 20th-century American art; includes works by Calder, Dove, de Kooning, Lichtenstein, Nevelson, Pollock, Rothko, Stella, Warhol. **Highlights:** Bellows, *Dempsey and Firpo;* Calder, *Circus;* Hartley, *Painting, Number 5;* Henri, *Gertrude Vanderbilt Whitney;* Hopper, *Early Sunday Morning;* Johns, *Three Flags;* Lachaise, *Standing Woman;* Nadelman, *Tango.* **Architecture:** 1966 building by Breuer; addition by Graves planned.

Admission
Adults $4.50; seniors $2.50; students with ID & children under 12 accompanied by adult free. Tues., 6–8, free. Handicapped accessible; wheelchairs available.

Hours
Tues., 1–8; Wed.–Sat., 11–5; Sun., noon–6. Closed Mon. & national holidays.

Tours
Tues.–Fri. at 1:30 & 3:30; Sat.–Sun. at 2:30 & 3:30. Call (212) 606-0395 for information.

Food & Drink
Restaurant: Tues., 1–7; Wed.–Sat., 11:30–4:30; Sun., noon–5.

Whitney Branches

at Equitable Center
787 Seventh Ave., New York, N.Y.

in Fairfield County
One Champion Plaza, Stamford, Conn.

at Federal Reserve Plaza
33 Maiden Lane, New York, N.Y.

at Philip Morris
120 Park Ave., New York, N.Y.

Other Collections of Note

American Craft Museum
40 West 53d St., New York, N.Y. 10019
(212) 956-6047

Newport Beach, Calif.

The Grey Art Gallery and Study Center
33 Washington Pl., New York, N.Y. 10003
(212) 598-7603

International Center of Photography
1130 Fifth Ave., New York, N.Y. 10128
(212) 860-1777

Museum of American Folk Art
444 Park Ave. South, New York, N.Y. 10016
(212) 581-2474

The Pierpont Morgan Library
29 East 36th St., New York, N.Y. 10016
(212) 685-0008

The Studio Museum in Harlem
144 West 125th St., New York, N.Y. 10027
(212) 864-4500

Newport Harbor Art Museum

850 San Clemente Dr., Newport Beach, Calif. 92660
(714) 759-1122

1990 Exhibitions
Jan. 21–Mar. 18
Installation Art from the Permanent Collection

Jan. 21–Mar. 18
New California Artist XVII

Apr. 8–June 24
OBJECTives: The New Sculpture
Art of a group of American and European sculptors whose work has been described as "New Object" or "Neogeo."

July 15–Sept. 23
Charles Ray, Sculptor
Explores territory between sculpture, installation, and performance art.

July 15–Sept. 23
Committed to Print

July 15–Sept. 23
New California Artist XVIII

Oct. 14–Dec. 30
Tony Cragg
The first major U.S. exhibition of the British sculptor and recent winner of the Turner Award.

Installation Plan: Connections, 1981, by Barry Le Va. Newport Harbor Art Museum.

Norfolk, Va.

Permanent Collection
Post-1945 California art. **Highlights:** Work by Baldessari, Bengston, Burden, Celmins, Diebenkorn, Goode, Ruscha. Room-size installations by Burden, Kienholz, Stone, Viola. **Architecture:** Opened in 1977; 1993 building by Piano planned.

Admission
Adults $3; seniors, military with ID, students with ID $2; children, 6–17, $1.

Hours
Tues.–Sun., 10–5. Handicapped accessible.

Tours
Tues.–Fri., 12:15, 1:15; Sat.–Sun. at 2. For group tours call (714) 759-1122.

Food & Drink
Sculpture Garden Café: Mon.–Fri., 11:30–2:30.

The Chrysler Museum

**Olney Rd. & Mowbray Arch, Norfolk, Va. 23510
(804) 622-1211; 622-ARTS (recorded)**

1990 Exhibitions
Thru Jan. 7
Eadweard Muybridge
Displays the photographer's noted images of motion studies, used widely as references by artists.

Jan. 26–Apr. 8
The Portrait in America
Portraits by photographers Hawes, Mapplethorpe, Southworth, Steichen, studio of Mathew Brady, and Ulmann.

Apr. 21–June 24
Life's Lessons by Bea Nettles
An autobiographical installation made with Polaroid images.

Feb. 9–Apr. 8
Prophets and Translators for the New Decade: Four Black Artists
Works by Colescott, Conwill, Pindell, and Ringgold reflect contemporary viewpoints and African-American roots.

May 11–July 8
American Modernist Painters from The Phillips Collection
Includes works by Bluemner, Demuth, Dove, Hartley, Marin, Marsden, Maurer, O'Keeffe.

May 13–July 8
The Thirtieth Annual Irene Leache Memorial Exhibition

Northampton, Mass.

July 3–Sept. 2
Light Images 1990
Winners of a Virginia photography competition.

July 28–Sept. 16
The Art of Babar
Presents about 150 watercolors by Jean de Brunhoff and his son Laurent, creators of the well-known Babar stories.

Oct. 12–Dec. 23
Alexander Gardner
First retrospective of Gardner's Civil War photographs; features the last portrait of Lincoln and the only portraits of the Lincoln conspirators.

Permanent Collection
Art of many civilizations, styles, and historical periods: Ancient Greek and Roman works; Pre-Columbian and African textiles and ceramics; Asian bronzes; American 19th-century sculpture; contemporary painting and sculpture; glassware. **Highlights:** Bernini, *Bust of the Savior;* Cassatt, *The Family;* Gauguin, *The Loss of Innocence;* La Tour, *Saint Philip;* Lichtenstein, *Live Ammo (Fifth Panel);* Matisse, *Bowl of Apples;* Rouault, *Head of Christ;* Veronese, *The Virgin Appearing to Saints Anthony Abbott and Paul the Hermit.* **Architecture:** 1933 building; 1967 Houston Wing; 1976 Centennial Wing; 1989 renovation and expansion by Hartman-Cox.

Bowl of Apples, 1916, by Henri Matisse. The Chrysler Museum.

Admission
Donation suggested: $2. Handicapped accessible.

Hours
Tues.–Sat., 10–4; Sun., 1–5. Closed Mon., Jan. 1, July 4, Thanksgiving, Dec. 25.

Tours
Sun. at 2 & 3; Wed. at 2.

Food & Drink
Café: Tues.–Sat., 10–4; Sun., 1–5

Smith College Museum of Art

Elm St. at Bedford Terr., Northampton, Mass. 01063
(413) 584-2700, ext. 2760

1990 Exhibitions
Thru Feb. 18
Baroque Drawings and Prints
Includes works by Carracci, Ribera, Rosa, and others.

Northampton, Mass.

The Walking Man, present cast 1965 (conceived 1877–78, first cast 1907), by Auguste Rodin. Smith College Museum of Art.

Thru Feb. 18
Baroque Painters in Italy
Over 40 works by Ribera and little known women painters Fetti, Gentileschi, and Sirani demonstrate the diversity of styles and subjects in this dynamic period.

Feb. 3–Mar. 25
Dimensions of Discovery: Selections from the Cecilia and Irwin Smiley Collection of African Sculpture
Works from the major Sub-Saharan stylistic regions. Catalogue.

Mar. 1–May 20
An Installation by Nancy Spero
A mural expresses contemporary concerns of women with images inspired by ancient Egypt, classical Greece and Rome, the ancient Celts, the Vietnam War, and the artist's own private mythology.

Mar. 15–May 20
Northampton/Postcards
Images by twelve noted contemporary photographers commissioned by the museum; a selection will be published as postcards. Brochure.

Mar. 27–May 20
Yvonne Jacquette: Prints
First exhibition of prints by the contemporary realist known for her luminous nocturnal cityscapes and aerial views. Catalogue.

May 21–Early Fall
Closed for renovation.

Permanent Collection
Emphasis on 18th- to 20th-century French and American paintings, sculptures, prints, drawings, watercolors, photographs, decorative arts. **Highlights:** Late Roman head of Emperor Gallienus; Bouts, *Portrait of a Young Man;* Courbet, *La Toilette de la Mariée;* Degas, *Jephthah's Daughter;* Eakins, *Mrs. Edith Mahon;* Elmer, *Mourning Picture;* Lehmbruck, *Torso of the Pensive Woman;* Rembrandt, *The Three Crosses;* Rodin, *Walking Man;* Sheeler, *Rolling Power;* Terbrugghen, *Old Man Writing by Candlelight.* **Architecture:** 1973 building by Andrews.

Admission
Free. Handicapped accessible.

Hours
Tues.–Sat., 12–5; Sun., 2–5. Closed Mon.

Tours
Call (413) 585-2760 for information.

Oakland Museum

**1000 Oak St., Oakland, Calif. 94607
(415) 273-3401; 834-2413 (recorded)**

1990 Exhibitions

Thru Jan. 7
Diamonds Are Forever: Artists and Writers on Baseball
Features paintings, photographs, and drawings that reflect on baseball as a national inspiration.

Thru Jan. 7
Fit for America: Health, Fitness, Sport, and American Society, 1830–1940

Thru Jan. 28
Birds of South San Francisco Bay Wetlands
Photographs by Thomas Rountree.

Thru Feb. 18
Beatrice Wood: Intimate Appeal
Features figurative drawings and sculptures.

Feb. 2–Apr. 15
Stitching Memories: African American Story Quilts

Feb. 17–May
Strength and Diversity: Japanese American Women
Historical exploration of three generations through artifacts, photographs, and texts.

Mar. 24–July
Oakland Artists 1990

Apr. 14–June 17
Jack Zajac/Sculpture

Aug. 18–Oct. 15
Colors and Impressions: The Early Work of E. C. Fortune

Aug. 18–Nov. 11
Folk Roots, New Roots: Folklore in American Life

Oct. 13–Dec. 16
Against the Grain: Early Los Angeles Modernists

Permanent Collection
Works by California artists dating from the earliest explorers; artifacts from the Indian era, Spanish-American period, Anglo-American period; Californiana.
Architecture: 1969 building by Roche.

Admission
Free. Handicapped accessible.

Omaha, Nebr.

Hours
Wed.–Sat., 10–5; Sun., noon–7. Closed Mon.–Tues., Jan. 1, July 4, Dec. 25.

Tours
Wed.–Fri. at 2; first & third Sun. of month at 1. Call (415) 273-3514 for information.

Food & Drink
Snack Bar: Wed.–Sat., 10–4; Sun., noon–5.

Joslyn Art Museum

**2200 Dodge St., Omaha, Nebr. 68102
(402) 342-3300**

1990 Exhibitions
Thru Feb. 4
Forty Years of California Assemblage
Various works trace the history of assemblage from dada and surrealism to the present day.

Feb. 24–Apr. 8
Virtue Rewarded: Victorian Paintings from the Forbes Magazine Collection

Apr. 21–June 24
†*Jim Dine Drawings*
First comprehensive exhibition of the master draftsman's recent drawings.

The Vintage at Château Lagrange, 1864, by Jules Breton. Joslyn Art Museum.

Permanent Collection
Works from antiquity to the present. Major holdings of 19th- and 20th-century European and American art; Native American art; works by artist-explorers Bodmer, Catlin, Miller, Remington, documenting the movement to the American West. **Highlights:** Degas, *Little Dancer, Fourteen Years Old;* Pollock, *Galaxy;* Renoir, *Two Girls at the Piano;* Segal, *Times Square at Night;* Titian, *Man with a Falcon;* sculpture garden; Storz Fountain Court. **Architecture:** 1931 art deco building by John and Alan McDonald.

Admission
Adults $2; seniors & children under 12 $1. Sat., 10–noon, free. Handicapped accessible.

Hours
Tues.–Sat., 10–5; Thurs., 10–9; Sun., 1–5. Closed Mon. & holidays.

Tours
Wed. at 1. Call (402) 342-3300 for information.

Food & Drink
Gallery Buffet: Tues.–Fri., 11:30–2.

Pasadena, Calif.

Norton Simon Museum

411 West Colorado Blvd., Pasadena, Calif. 91105
(818) 449-6840; 449-3730

1990 Exhibitions
Features special exhibitions from the permanent collection.

Permanent Collection
Renaissance, baroque, and 18th-century paintings by Botticelli, Fragonard, Raphael, Rembrandt, Rubens, Watteau, Zurbarán; 19th-century works by Cézanne, van Gogh, Goya, Monet, Renoir; 20th-century art by Brancusi, Klee, Lehmbruck, Lipchitz, Maillol, Matisse, Picasso, Rodin; Indian and Southeast Asian sculpture. **Highlights:** Canaletto, *Piazzetta, Venice, Looking North;* bronzes by Degas; Raphael, *Madonna;* Reni, *Saint Cecilia;* Rubens, *The Holy Women at the Sepulcher;* Ruisdael landscapes; Steen, *Wedding Feast at Cana;* Zurbarán, *Still Life with Lemons, Oranges, and a Rose;* sculpture gardens. **Architecture:** 1969 building by Ladd; 1974 renovation.

Admission
Adults $3; seniors & students $1.50; children under 12 free. Handicapped accessible.

Hours
Thurs.–Sun., noon–6. Closed Mon.–Wed., Jan. 1 Thanksgiving, Dec. 1.

Tours
Call (818) 449-6840 for information.

Institute of Contemporary Art

University of Pennsylvania, 34th & Walnut Sts., Philadelphia, Pa. 19104
(215) 898-7108

1990 Exhibitions
Thru Jan. 28
Francesca Woodman
A representative selection of the artist's work, including photographs and large-scale blueprints.

Thru Jan. 28
Ilya Kabakov
Features a mixedmedia installation by the Soviet artist in his first solo U.S. exhibition.

Philadelphia, Pa.

Mar. 9–Apr. 29
Art as Artifact
Installations, paintings, photographs, and sculptures by 15 artists who attempt to define with singleminded conviction the individual's relationship to nature.

June 8–July 29
Investigations 1990
An ongoing series featuring emerging or critically neglected artists, new work by established artists, and current themes and issues in the visual arts.

Permanent Collection
No permanent collection. **Architecture:** 1990 building planned.

Admission
Adults $2; artists, seniors, students over 12 $1; children under 12 free. Wed., free. Handicapped accessible.

Hours
Mon.–Tues., Sat.–Sun., 10–5; Wed. & Fri., 10–8. Summer: Daily, noon–5.

Tours
Call (215) 898-7108 for information.

Pennsylvania Academy of the Fine Arts

Broad & Cherry Sts., Philadelphia, Pa. 19102
(215) 972-7600

1990 Exhibitions
Feb. 2–Apr. 15
Paris 1889: American Artists at the Universal Exposition
Features paintings by American and European artists who exhibited at the 1889 World's Fair in Paris. Artists include Chase, Eakins, Sargent, Whistler.

May 10–June 3
Annual Student Exhibition
Over 400 works by third- and fourth-year students at the School of the Pennsylvania Academy of the Fine Arts.

June 8–Apr. 14, 1991
Light, Color, and Air: American Impressionism at the Pennsylvania Academy of the Fine Arts

June 16–Sept. 23
Sculptures by Duane Hanson

The Cello Player, 1896, by Thomas Eakins. Pennsylvania Academy of the Fine Arts.

Oct. 5–Dec. 30
†*Bay Area Figurative Art, 1950–1965*
A definitive look at the postwar expressionist impulse as manifested on the West Coast, with works by Bischoff, Brown, Diebenkorn, Neri, Oliveira, Park. Catalogue.

Permanent Collection
Paintings, sculptures, and works on paper spanning more than three centuries of American art. **Highlights:** Benbridge, *The Gordon Family;* Diebenkorn, *Interior with Doorway;* Eakins, *Portrait of Walt Whitman;* Graves, *Hay Fever;* Henri, *Ruth St. Denis in the Peacock Dance;* Hicks, *The Peaceable Kingdom;* Homer, *The Fox Hunt;* Peale, *The Artist in His Museum;* Pippin, *John Brown Going to His Hanging;* Rush, *Self-Portrait;* West, *Death on a Pale Horse*; Wyeth, *Young America.* **Architecture:** 1876 High-Victorian Gothic-style building by Furness and Hewitt; 1976 restoration declared a national historic landmark.

Admission
Adults $5; seniors $3; students $2; members, children under 5 free. Sat., 10–1, free. Handicapped accessible.

Hours
Tues.–Sat., 10–5; Sun., 11–5. Closed Mon. & holidays.

Tours
Tues.–Fri. at 11 & 2; Sat.–Sun. at 2. Call (215) 972-7608 for information.

Philadelphia Museum of Art

26th St. & Benjamin Franklin Pkwy.,
Philadelphia, Pa. 19130
(215) 763-8100

1990 Exhibitions
Thru Jan. 7
Perpetual Motif: The Art of Man Ray
Demonstrates the significance of the 20th-century artist and photographer whose thematic explorations in diverse media anticipated the cross-disciplinary concerns of many of today's artists. Catalogue.

Thru Feb. 11
Nineteenth-Century French Etchings from the Collections

Feb. 10–Mar. 25
Recent Acquisitions of Costumes and Textiles, 1979–1989
Includes 17th- and 18th-century pieces.

Mar. 3–May 6
Joseph Sudek: A Life's Work
Vintage prints by the late Czech photographer.

Philadelphia, Pa.

Apr. 22–July 8
Contemporary Philidelphia Artists: A Juried Exhibition

Sept. 16–Nov. 25
Francesco Clemente: Works on Paper

Oct. 14–Jan. 15, 1991
Henry Ossawa Tanner
A retrospective of one of America's major black artists.

Nov. 2–Nov. 5
Philadelphia Craft Show

Permanent Collection
Significant works from many periods, styles, and cultures in diverse media. Architectural installations, including a 12th-century French Romanesque facade and portal, Spanish cloisters, 14th-century Japanese Buddhist temple, 16th-century carved granite Hindu temple hall; 17th-century Chinese palace hall; Japanese tea house and temple. Period rooms, including Het Scheepje (The Little Ship), a 17th-century Dutch domestic interior; Robert Adams's drawing room from Lansdowne House. Modern sculpture with major Brancusi collection; German folk art; Kretzschmar von Kienbusch collection of arms and armor. **Highlights:** Cézanne, *Large Bathers;* Duchamp, *Nude Descending a Staircase;* van Eyck, *Saint Francis Receiving the Stigmata;* van Gogh, *Sunflowers;* Picasso, *The Three Musicians;* Poussin, *Birth of Venus;* Renoir, *The Bathers;* Rubens, *Prometheus Bound;* Saint-Gaudens, *Diana;* van der Weyden, *Crucifixion with the Virgin and Saint John.* **Architecture:** 1928 replica of a Grecian temple by Abele, Borie, Trumbauer, and Zantzinger; 1940 Oriental Wing.

Admission
Adults $5; seniors, students with ID, children $2.50. Sun., 10–1, free. Handicapped accessible; wheelchairs available.

Hours
Tues.–Sun., 10–5. Closed Mon. & holidays.

Tours
Call (215) 787-5498 for information.

Food & Drink
Restaurant: Tues.–Sun., 11:45–2:15. Cafeteria: Tues.–Fri., 10–3:30; Sat.–Sun., 11–3:45.

Philadelphia Museum of Art Branches:

The Rodin Museum
22d St. & Benjamin Franklin Parkway,
Philadelphia, Pa. 19104
(215) 763-8100

Silent Harp, 1944, by Man Ray. From *Perpetual Motif: The Art of Man Ray* at the Philadelphia Museum of Art, thru Jan. 7.

Other Collections of Note

The Barnes Foundation
300 North Latch's Lane, Merion Station, Pa. 19066
(near Philadelphia)
(215) 667-0290

The University Museum of Archaeology and Anthropology, University of Pennsylvania,
33d & Spruce Sts., Philadelphia, Pa. 19104
(215) 898-4000

Phoenix Art Museum

1625 North Central Ave., Phoenix, Ariz. 85004
(602) 257-1222

1990 Exhibitions
Jan. 13–Apr. 8
Frank Lloyd Wright Drawings
Features 300 of the architect's works.

May 5–June 17
Graphic Design in America: A Visual Language History
Explores the aesthetic and social evolution of graphic design with works by Bass, Bayer, Chermayeff, Wurman, and others. Catalogue.

May 26–Aug. 5
Yixing Teaware

July 7–Aug. 19
L.A. Pop in the Sixties
Features major works by Baldessari, Bengston, Celmins, Dowd, Foulkes, Goode, Hefferton, Ruscha.

Sept. 8–Oct. 7
1990 Phoenix Triennial
Artwork created over the last three years in southern California, Arizona, New Mexico, and Texas.

Oct. 27–Nov. 18
Cowboy Artists of America
Includes paintings and bronze sculptures.

Permanent Collection
Western American art; 19th- and 20th-century American, European, and Mexican art; Chinese, Japanese, and Indian art, including fine porcelains and paintings; costumes from 1750 to the present. **Highlights:** Archipenko, *Kimono;* Bengston, *Dodge City.* Exquisitely detailed miniature period rooms illustrating American, English, French, and Italian interiors.

Pittsburgh, Pa.

Admission
Adults $3; seniors & students $2.50; children under 13 free. Wed., free, donation suggested. Handicapped accessible.

Hours
Tues.–Sat., 10–5; Wed., 10–9; Sun., 1–5. Closed Mon. & holidays.

Tours
Tues.–Sun. at 1:30; Wed. at 7. Call (602) 257-1880.

Other Collections of Note

**The Heard Museum (Native American Collections)
22 East Monte Vista Rd., Phoenix, Ariz. 85004
(602) 252-8848**

The Carnegie

**4400 Forbes Ave., Pittsburgh, Pa. 15213
(412) 622-3313**

1990 Exhibitions
Thru Jan. 14
Ross Bleckner
Includes about 15 paintings reflecting the decade's preoccupations with AIDS and nuclear war.

Thru Feb. 4
The Japanese Print and the Impressionist Vision
Japanese prints address the art form's influence on European art during the late 18th to 19th centuries.

Jan. 20–Mar. 18
Marcel Broodthaers
Features about 200 works from the Belgian artist and poet's short but prolific career, including sculptures, paintings, films, slide projections, and installations.

Apr. 14–June 10
The American Craftsmen and the European Tradition, 1620–1820
Includes furniture, ceramics, glass, and silver.

Permanent Collection
French impressionist and postimpressionist paintings; 19th- and 20th-century American art; European and American furniture and decorative art; European silver and porcelain; oriental and African art. **Highlights:** D'Ancona, *Madonna and Child;* Bonnard, *Nude in Bathtub;* Cassatt, *Young Woman Picking Fruit;* van Gogh, *Plain of Auvers;* Homer, *The Wreck;* de Kooning, *Woman VI;* Monet, *Water Lily;* Smith, *Cubi XXIV;* monumental architectural casts; film and video program; sculpture court. **Architecture:** 1896–1907

beaux-arts building; Hall of Sculpture designed to resemble the cella of the Parthenon.

Admission
Adults $4; students & children $2. Handicapped accessible; wheelchairs available; call (412) 662-3343.

Hours
Tues.–Sat., 10–5; Fri., 10–9; Sun., 1–5. Closed Mon. & holidays.

Tours
Call (412) 622-3289.

Food & Drink
Café: Tues.–Sat., 10–3; Sun., 1–4.

Oregon Art Institute

1219 S.W. Park Ave., Portland, Oreg. 97205
(503) 226-2811

1990 Exhibitions
Thru Jan. 28
Views of Edo
Works by such artists as Eishi, Hiroshige, and Hokusai along with several early scenes of Kabuki theater interiors.

Thru Feb. 4
New Look to Now: French Couture, 1947–1987
Features designs by Balenciaga, Balmain, Chanel, Courreges, Dior, Gres, Saint Laurent, and others.

Mar. 20–Apr. 22
Summoning of the Souls: Treasures from the Tombs of China
Explores life in Han dynasty China (12th–2d century B.C.) through silks, lacquerware, and wooden tomb figurines excavated at the tomb of the marquis of Dai at Mawangdui in Hunan province. Catalogue.

Apr. 24–June 1
Piranesi
Piranese's skill as an etcher and mastery of light, depth, and atmosphere are revealed in his richly detailed depictions of ancient vases, imaginary prison scenes, and etchings from his Views of Rome series.

May 1–June 8
Contemporary Art from the Collection

Nov. 16–Dec. 31
Northwest Viewpoints: Dennis Cunningham–Fish Tales
Collage-like compositions and linocut block prints.

Princeton, N.J.

To be announced
Perspectives 14: "Doug Hall: The Terrible Uncertainty of the Thing Described"
Video installation presents nature in a state of turmoil, accompanied by audio tracks and a Tesla coil that periodically sends bolts of low-level electricity arching across the gallery.

Permanent Collection
19th- and 20th-century works; Northwest Indian art; Kress collection of Renaissance and baroque paintings; Cameroon sculptures. **Highlights:** Pre-Han Standing Horse; Brancusi, *Muse;* Monet, *Water Lilies;* Renoir, *Two Girls Reading;* Tlingit Wolf Hat. **Architecture:** 1932 building by Belluschi; 1989 renovation.

Admission
Adults $3; seniors & students $1.50; children, 6–12, 50¢; children under 6 free; first Thurs. of month, 5–9:30, free. Handicapped accessible.

Hours
Tues.–Fri., 11–7; Thurs., 11–9:30; Sat.–Sun., noon–5. Closed Mon.

Tours
Call (503) 226-2811 for information.

Food & Drink
Restaurant: Open during museum hours.

The Art Museum, Princeton University

Princeton, N.J. 08544-1018
(609) 258-3788

Drinking Contest between Dionysos and Herakles, early third century A.D., Roman. The Art Museum, Princeton University.

1990 Exhibitions
Feb. 10–Mar. 11
Winslow Homer

Sept. 22–Nov. 18
From Athens to Alexandria: Greek Terracottas of the Hellenistic Period

Permanent Collection
One of the oldest college and university museums in the country featuring European painting, sculpture, decorative arts. **Highlights:** Allori, *Penitent Saint Jerome;* Benbridge, *Portrait of the Hartley Family;* Carracci, *Kiss of Judas;* Conca, *The Baptism of Christ;* Eakins, *A Singer;* Homer, *At the Window;* Linnell, *Job and the Messengers;* Po, *The Sleep of Adam and Eve* and *The Gates of Hell;* Rosa, *The Angel Leaving the House of Tobias.* **Architecture:** 1890

Romanesque building by Brown; 1921 Venetian Gothic McCormick Hall by Cram; 1966 entrance, gallery space, library, and auditorium by Steinmann and Cain; 1985 Mitchell Wolfson, Jr., Wing and 1989 building with sky-lit court by Mitchell/Giurgola.

Admission
Free. Handicapped accessible.

Hours
Tues.–Sat., 10–5; Sun., 1–5. Closed Mon. & major holidays.

Tours
By reservation only: Groups under 20, $35; groups over 20, $50; children and school groups free. Call (609) 258-3762 or Tues.–Thurs., 11–2, (609) 258-3043.

Museum of Art, Rhode Island School of Design

224 Benefit St., Providence, R.I. 02903
(401) 331-3511

1990 Exhibitions
Thru Feb. 4
The Art of the Poster, 1870–1920
Includes work by Brangwyn, Chéret, Pennell, Steinlen, Sterner, Toulouse-Lautrec.

Jan. 19–Mar. 18
Contemporary Crafts from the Permanent Collection
Features works in ceramics, glass, metal, textiles, and furniture by Bean, Chihuly, Gill, Gustin, Kraus, Mueller, Prip, Tre, and others.

Jan. 19–Apr. 22
The Landscape Tradition
A selection of landscape prints from the 15th through the 19th centuries, ranging from artists Dürer to Dix.

Jan. 19–Apr. 22
Terra Incognita
Explores the traditional landscape ranging from the conceptual to the abstract by contemporary painters Deutsch, Long, Steir, and Stuart.

Feb. 16–May 20
Three Centuries of Architectural and Decorative Drawings
Works from the early 18th–late 20th century; includes work by American architects Everett, Flagg, Laud, and Peabody from their studies at the Ecole des Beaux-arts in Paris.

May 18–June 3
RISD Graduate Students

Richmond, Va.

June 15–July 1
Schoolart

Permanent Collection
Greek and Roman art; Asian art; masterpieces of European, American painting and sculpture from the early Middle Ages to the present; French impressionist painting; Ameri-can furniture and decorative art. **Architecture:** Includes the Pendleton House, first decorative arts wing built in the U.S.

Admission
Adults $1; seniors 50¢; children, 5–18, 25¢. Thurs., 6–8, & Sat., free. Handicapped accessible.

Hours
Tues.–Wed. & Fri.–Sat., 10:30–5; Thurs., noon–8; Sun., 2–5. Closed Mon., Jan. 1, July 4, Thanksgiving, Dec. 25.

Tours
Call (401) 331-3511, ext. 349.

Virginia Museum of Fine Arts

2800 Grove Ave., Richmond, Va. 23221-2466
(804)367-0844

1990 Exhibitions
Jan. 23–Mar. 4
American Painting from a Century of Collecting: The Maier Museum of Art, Randolph-Macon Woman's College
The evolution of American art through the early 19th century is illustrated in 50 works by Chase, Cole, Davies, Dove, Durand, Kensett, Marin, O'Keeffe, Robinson, and Twachtman. Catalogue.

Jan. 30–Mar. 11
Chris Silliman–Recent Sculpture

Jan. 30–Mar. 11
David E. Thompson–Recent Sculpture

Feb. 1–Apr. 22
The Consul Smith Collection: Raphael to Canaletto
Presents 60 masterpiece drawings from Windsor Castle.

Feb. 2–Apr. 29
Holy Image, Holy Space: Icons and Frescoes from Greece
About 80 early Byzantine works gathered from all over Greece. Catalogue.

Apr. 3–May 13
Landscape: An American Vision Today
Paintings by contemporary U.S. and Virginia artists.

Apr. 25–June 17
Vanishing Presence
Displays 19th- and 20th-century photographs using time exposures, multiple exposures, blurred effects. Catalogue.

May 22–July
Selections from the Goode Design Collection of the Virginia Museum of Fine Arts

June 5–July 15
Robert Stackhouse/Installation and Related Drawings

June 19–Aug. 19
Wendell Castle: A Retrospective
Surveys the work of the contemporary American sculptor who challenges traditional concepts of furniture design. Catalogue.

Aug. 22–Nov. 25
†*The Romance of the Taj Mahal*
Presents the world-famous monument through models, prints, drawings, and paintings by Indian and British artists; also includes gems, jewelry, carpets, textiles. Catalogue.

Oct. 23–Dec. 16
Un/Common Ground: Virginia Artists 1990

Black and White Spaniel Following a Scent, 1773, by George Stubbs. Virginia Musum of Fine Arts.

Permanent Collection
Comprehensive holdings dating from ancient times to the present: Byzantine, medieval, African art; Indian, Nepalese, Tibetan art; American paintings since World War II; art nouveau and art deco works. **Highlights:** Statue of Caligula; Mellon collections of English sporting art and French impressionist and postimpressionist works; Fabergé Easter eggs from the Russian imperial collection; Gobelin Don Quixote tapestries; Goya, *General Nicolas Guye;* Monet, *Irises by the Pond;* sculpture garden. **Architecture:** 1936 building by Peebles and Ferguson; 1954 addition by Lee; 1970 addition by Baskerville & Son; 1976 addition by Hardwicke Associates; 1985 addition by Holzman.

Admission
Donation suggested: Adults $2; seniors, members, children free. Handicapped accessible.

Hours
Tues.–Sat., 11–5; Thurs., 11–10; Sun., 1–5. Closed Mon., Jan. 1, July 4, Thanksgiving, Dec. 25.

Tours
Tues.–Sat., hourly, 11:30–2:30; Thurs. walk-in tours at 6 & 7; Sun. at 2 & 3. For reservations call (804) 367-0859 two weeks in advance.

Food & Drink
Arts Café: Tues.–Sat., 11:30–2:30; Sun., 1–4. Tea in the Renaissance Court: Sat. & Sun., 2:30–4:30.

Sacramento, Calif.

Crocker Art Museum

216 O St., Sacramento, Calif. 95814
(916) 449-5423

1990 Exhibitions

Thru Jan. 7
Images of Reality, Images of Arcadia: Seventeenth-Century Netherlandish Paintings from Swiss Collections
Features over 40 works of northern Renaissance art by Claesz, Hobbema, van Ostade, van Ruisdael, and others.

Thru Aug.
Highlights of the Early California Painting Collection
Paintings by Bierstadt, Browere, Deakin, Denny, Hahn, Hill, Keith, Nahl, Ritschel, Welch.

Jan. 28–Mar. 25
*Lartigue: Panoramas of the Twenties
Forty images, 1922–30, reveal the photographer's fascination with motion and speed, featuring automobile races, glider launchings, and people diving into pools.

Apr. 20–June 4
Sixty-fifth Annual Crocker-Kingsley Exhibition
Presents a cross-section of current work by Northern and Central California artists.

June 23–Aug. 25
A Vision of Light and Color
Paintings, photographs, and other memorabilia explore the theme of light and color in American art; features artists Bischoff, Clark, Kleitsch, Rose. Catalogue.

Dec. 9–Feb. 3, 1991
†*Of Time and the City: American Modernism from the Sheldon Memorial Art Gallery*
Features assemblages, collages, drawings, paintings, prints, sculptures, watercolors. Catalogue.

Permanent Collection

Babylonian tablets; Asian art, including Korean pottery; Pre-Columbian ceramics; old master paintings and drawings, including 19th-century German painting; European and American photography; 19th-century paintings by California artists Hahn, Hill, Keith, Nahl; contemporary Northern California art by Arneson, Brown, Raffael, Thiebaud, Voulkos, Wiley; American Victorian furniture and decorative arts; textiles. **Highlights:** Hill, *Great Canyon of the Sierras, Yosemite;* Nahl, *Sunday Morning in the Mines* and *The Fandango;* Thiebaud, *Boston Cremes.* **Architecture:** 1873 Crocker mansion by Barnes; 1969 Herold Wing; 1989 Crocker Mansion Wing and Pavilion.

Admission

Adults $2.50; seniors $1.50; children, 7–17, $1; children under 7 free. Handicapped accessible.

St. Louis, Mo.

Hours
Tues., 1–9; Wed.–Sun., 10–5. Closed Mon., Jan. 1, July 4, Thanksgiving, Dec. 25.

Tours
By reservation, Tues.–Thurs., 10–4; call (916) 449-5537 or 449-5423.

The Saint Louis Art Museum

Forest Park, St. Louis, Mo. 63110
(314) 721-0067

1990 Exhibitions
Thru Jan. 14
150 Years of Photography from St. Louis Collections
Presents a comprehensive history of photography.

Feb. 22–May 13
George Caleb Bingham
Focuses on the artist's great genre paintings. First major exhibition of his work in more than 20 years. Catalogue.

July 14–Sept. 9
†*Impressionism: Selections from Five American Museums*
Features 85 paintings and sculptures by the celebrated impressionists and postimpressionists Bonnard, Cassatt, Degas, van Gogh, Manet, Monet, Pissarro, Renoir.

Oct. 10–Nov. 25
Art of the Eighties: The Post Modern Surface
American and European paintings, drawings, and photographs of five stylistic tendencies.

Permanent Collection
Encompasses the art of many periods, styles, and cultures: African, Asian, Oceanic, American Indian, Pre-Columbian art; European old master paintings and drawings; American art from colonial times to the present; French impressionist and postimpressionist and German expressionist works; 20th-century European art; decorative arts, including six period rooms. **Highlights:** Chagall, *Temptation;* Fantin-Latour, *The Two Sisters;* van Goyen, *Skating on the Ice near Dordrecht;* Smith, *Cubi XIV;* Vasari, *Judith and Holofernes;* Stella, *Marriage of Reason and Squalor.* **Architecture:** 1904 building by Gilbert for the World's Fair; 1977 renovation by Hardy Holzman Pfeiffer Associates; 1980 South Wing by Howard, Needles, Tammen, and Bergendorff; 1988 West Wing renovation by SMP/Smith-Entzeroth.

Admission
Free. Wed.–Sat., entrance fee for selected exhibitions. Handicapped accessible; wheelchairs available.

St. Petersburg, Fla.

Hours
Tues., 1:30–8:30; Wed.–Sun., 10–5. Closed Mon., Jan. 1, Thanksgiving, Dec. 25.

Tours
Thirty-minute tour, Wed.–Fri. at 1:30; 60-minute tour, Sat.–Sun. at 1:30.

Food & Drink
Museum Café: Lunch, snacks, cocktails; Tues., dinner.

Museum of Fine Arts

**255 Beach Dr. N.E., St. Petersburg, Fla. 33701-3498
(813) 896-2667**

1990 Exhibitions

Thru Jan. 28
Special Delivery: Murals for the New Deal Era
Designs and preliminary studies for federal buildings commissioned by the Roosevelt administration, 1934–43.

Thru Feb. 18
Majolica Ware from Southern Collections
About 50 objects illustrate the variety of technical effects and diversity of styles found in Italian majolica.

Thru Feb. 25
Swimmers
Features black-and-white and color images by internationally recognized photographers. Catalogue.

Thru Mar. 4
Illuminated Manuscripts from Four Florida Collections

Feb. 4–Feb. 18
Miniature Art
Fifteenth international show organized by the Miniature Art Society of Florida.

Mar. 11–May 6
†*Gari Melchers: A Retrospective*
First significant exhibition since 1938 of the work of the famed Detroit artist. Catalogue.

Mar. 11–June 3
English Creamware c. 1760–1810: Fifty Years of Fashion and Fancy

May 15–July 8
Fact and Fiction: The State of Florida Photography
A comprehensive selection of images by photographers working in Florida. Catalogue.

Wasserburg on the Inn, 1907, by Alexej von Jawlensky. Museum of Fine Arts.

St. Petersburg, Fla.

May 15–July 8
Three Latin American Artists

June–July
A. Aubrey Bodine: Baltimore Pictorialist, 1906–1970
Features vintage images by the photographer who worked for the Baltimore Sunday Sun. 1927–70.

July 3–Aug. 26
The Tactile Vessel: New Basket Forms
Contemporary American baskets crafted with leather, ribbon, waxed linen, and hog gut among other materials. Catalogue.

July 17–Aug. 26
Frederick Waugh: Majesty in Motion
Presents 40 marine paintings from the Frederick Waugh Collection of Wichita State University, Kansas.

Sept. 4–Oct. 14
Five Centuries of Italian Painting: 1300–1800
Features 49 works by Botticelli, Tiepolo, Tintoretto, and Veronese, among others.

Sept. 4–Nov. 18
Glass from the Billups Collection: The New Orleans Museum of Art
Eighty masterworks ranging from ancient through art deco; includes classical mosaic fragments, cosmetic containers, rare early European pieces.

Oct. 30–Dec. 9
Florence Putterman: 1970–1990
Retrospective of recent works by the celebrated Florida painter and printmaker.

Dec. 18–Feb. 3, 1991
Dutch and Flemish Old Master Paintings from the Collection of Dr. and Mrs. Gordon Gilbert

Dec. 18–Mar. 17, 1991
Opulent Georgian and Victorian Jewels: The Collection of Nancy and Gilbert Levine
Illustrates jewelry design from 1790–1900. Catalogue.

Permanent Collection
Pre-Columbian gold and pottery; notable ancient and Far Eastern collection; 17th- to 20th-century European and American paintings and sculpture, including French impressionist paintings; 19th- and 20th-century photographs, prints, decorative arts. **Highlights:** Barye, *War;* Boudin, *Laundresses on the Shore of La Touques;* O'Keeffe, *Poppy;* Steuben glass gallery; Weenix, *The De Kempenaer Family;* Jacobean and Georgian period rooms. **Architecture:** 1965 Palladian-style building by Volk; 1989 expansion by Harvard, Jolly, Marcet, and Associates.

San Diego, Calif.

Admission
Donation suggested: $2. Handicapped accessible.

Hours
Tues.–Sat., 10–5; Sun., 1–5; third Thurs. of month, 10–9. Closed Mon., Jan. 1, Dec. 25.

Tours
Tues.–Fri. at 11 & 2; Sat.–Sun. at 2. Call (813) 896-2667 for group and Spanish-language tour reservations.

San Diego Museum of Art

1450 El Prado, Balboa Park, San Diego, Calif. 92101
(619) 232-7931

Museum Facade, San Diego Museum of Art.

1990 Exhibitions
Thru Jan. 7
Fabergé: The Imperial Eggs
The largest collection of Fabergé imperial eggs ever assembled for public viewing.

Jan. 27–Mar. 11
Artists Guild Annual Juried Exhibition

Mar. 10–Apr. 22
Young Art '90
Exhibit of student work.

June 23–Sept. 30
Frank Lloyd Wright: In The Realm of Ideas
Includes large-scale models, furniture, drawings, photographs, and a full-scale Usonian Automatic House.

Nov. 10–Jan. 6, 1991
Art Nouveau

Permanent Collection
Indian and Persian paintings; Asian art, including Buddhist sculptures and ritual bronzes and Japanese prints; European painting and sculpture from the Renaissance to the 20th century, including notable Italian Renaissance, Dutch, and Spanish baroque art featuring works by Bosch, Bronzino, Giorgione, Veronese; American paintings by Chase, Eakins, Homer, O'Keeffe, Peale. **Highlights:** Beckmann, *Moon Landscape*; ter Borch, *The Love Letter;* Bougereau, *The Young Shepherdess;* Braque, *Still Life;* Rembrandt, *Young Man with a Cock's Feather in His Cap;* Rubens, *Allegory of Eternity;* Sanchez Cotán, *Quince, Cabbage, Melon, and Cucumber;* sculpture garden with works by Hepworth, Moore, Rickey, Rodin. **Architecture:** 1926 Plateresque-style building by Johnson and Snyder.

San Francisco, Calif.

Admission
Adults $5; seniors $4; military $3; students with ID & children, 6–18, $2; children under 6 free. Handicapped accessible.

Hours
Tues.–Sun., 10–4:30. Closed Mon., Jan. 1, Thanksgiving, Dec. 25.

Tours
Tues.–Thurs. at 10, 11, 1, 2; Fri.–Sun. at 1 & 2. Call (619) 232-7931 for information.

Food & Drink
Sculpture Garden Café: Tues.–Sun.

Other Collections of Note

Timken Art Gallery
1500 El Prado, Balboa Park, San Diego, Calif. 92101
(619) 239-5548

Asian Art Museum of San Francisco

The Avery Brundage Collection
Golden Gate Park, San Francisco, Calif. 94118
(415) 668-8921

1990 Exhibitions
Thru Feb. 4
Looking at Patronage: Recent Acquisitions of Asian Art
Chinese and Japanese paintings, Southeast Asian sculptures, a Korean burial tablet, Indian prints. Catalogue.

Thru June 17
Urban Archaeology: Chinatown Origins
More than 75 objects represent the most significant Gold Rush era find in Northern California, excavated from an early Chinese settlement in San Francisco's Chinatown.

Mar. 7–Apr. 29
Yani: The Brush of Innocence
Displays 69 works by the 14-year-old who began painting at the age of two and had her first exhibition at the age of four; includes many of her noted monkey paintings. Catalogue.

Mar. 14–Sept. 16
Women: Auspicious and Divine, Images of Southeast Asia and India
Features over 30 figurative works depicting the significant role of women in Buddhist and Hindu art.

Simhavaktra Dakini, 18th century A.D., Tibet. Asian Art Museum of San Francisco.

San Francisco, Calif.

July 4–Dec. 9
Qing Porcelains: From a Technical Point of View
Traces the technical advancement, experimentation, and innovation of Qing dynasty (1644–1912) porcelains.

Aug. 22–Oct. 28
Noble Prince: Bada Shanren and His Art
Calligraphy and painting by one of China's most enigmatic artists. Catalogue.

Sept. 26–Dec. 30
Brushstrokes
Traditional Chinese and Japonese calligraphy and painting.

Permanent Collection
Art of China, Japan, Korea, India, Southeast Asia, the Himalayas, the Near East: Sculptures, paintings, bronzes, jades, ceramics, textiles, decorative objects, architectural elements. **Highlights:** Newly reinstalled Himalayan gallery displaying objects from the permanent collection.

Admission
Adults $4; seniors & children, 12–17, $2; children under 12 free. Sat., 10–noon, and first Wed. & Sat. of month, free. Handicapped accessible; wheelchairs available.

Hours
Wed.–Sun., 10–5; first Wed. of month, 10–8:45. Closed Mon.–Tues. & holidays except July 4.

Tours
Call (415) 750-3638.

The Fine Arts Museums of San Francisco

**The California Palace of the Legion of Honor
Lincoln Park, near 34th Ave. & Clement St.,
San Francisco, Calif. 94121
(415) 750-3659 (recording)**

**The M. H. de Young Memorial Museum
Golden Gate Park, Eighth Ave. & JFK Dr.,
San Francisco, Calif. 94118
(415) 750-3659 (recording)**

1990 Exhibitions
Thru Jan. 21 (de Young)
Viewpoints X: Kongo Power Figures

Jan. 17–April 9 (de Young)
Viewpoints XI: Period Frames
Examines the construction, conservation, connoisseurship, and suitability of picture frames.

San Francisco, Calif.

Feb. 2–Apr. 4 (Legion of Honor)
Early American Photography: The First Fifty Years
A comprehensive showing of works by the 19th-century pioneers of American photography. Catalogue.

Mar. 10–June 17 (de Young)
Treasures of American Folk Art from the Abby Aldrich Rockefeller Folk Art Center
Features 18th- to 19th-century folk art objects including paints, fraktur, trade and shop signs, weather vanes, toys, decoys, quilts, coverlets. Catalogue.

Apr. 18–June 24 (de Young)
Viewpoints XII: Claude Lorrain

Apr. 18–July 1
†*Expressionism and Modern German Painting from the Thyssen-Bornemisza Collection*
Works from the distinguished family collection focusing on the movements of the Brück, Blaue Reiter, Bauhaus, and Neue Sachlichkeit. Includes works by Kandinsky, Kirchner, and Nolde. Catalogue.

Apr. 18–July 22 (Legion of Honor)
German Expressionist Works on Paper from the Achenbach Foundation for Graphic Arts

July 29–Oct. 7 (de Young)
†*Jim Dine Drawings*
First comprehensive exhibition of the master draftsman's recent drawings. Catalogue.

June 9–Sept. 3 (de Young)
Amish: The Art of the Quilt
Seventy-two quilts, 1870–1950, from the Esprit Collection.

July 5–Sept. 16 (de Young)
Eastman Johnson: "The Cranberry Harvest"
Displays Johnson's painting, studies and related works.

Sept.–Nov. (Legion of Honor)
Jasper Johns: Printed Symbols
Retrospective of the career of a major American artist—from *Target*, his first black-and-white lithograph (1960) to multicolored etchings (1987). Catalogue.

Sept. 27–Jan. 13, 1991 (de Young)
Viewpoints XIII: Ivory–Symbol of Excellence

Nov. 10–Jan. 27, 1991 (de Young)
The Art of Anatolian Kilims
The first comprehensive exhibition of pre-19th-century Anatolian kilims. Catalogue.

Dec. 8–Mar. 3, 1991 (Legion of Honor)
Rupert Garcia: Prints and Posters
Displays graphic work by an important Bay Area artist.

At the Milliner's, 1881, by Edouard Manet. The Fine Arts Museums of San Francisco.

San Francisco, Calif.

Permanent Collection
De Young: Arts of Oceania, Africa, the Americas; decorative arts; jewelry from the ancient world; Egyptian mummies. **Highlights:** Flemish tapestries; British paintings by Gainsborough, Reynolds, Romney; American paintings by Bingham, Church, Copley, Harnett, Sargent; Revere silver. **Architecture:** 1921 building by Mullgardt.

Legion of Honor: Kress collection of Renaissance and baroque painting; rococo paintings by Boucher and Watteau; Rodin sculptures including the earliest casting of *The Thinker.* **Highlights:** Fourteenth-century French tapestry, *The Apocalypse of Angers*; Cézanne, *Rocks in the Grounds of the Château Noir;* Fragonard, *Virgin and Child;* Rodin, *Saint John the Baptist;* installation of the Hôtel d'Humières in Paris. **Architecture:** 1924 neoclassical building duplicates building of same name in Paris.

Admission
Both museums: Adults $4; seniors & students $2; children under 12 free. First Wed. of month and first Sat. of month, 10–noon, free.

Hours
Wed.–Sun., 10–5. Closed Mon.–Tues.

Tours
Call (415) 750-3638.

Food & Drink
Café de Young & Café Chanticleer: Wed.–Sun., 10–4.

San Francisco Museum of Modern Art

401 Van Ness Ave., San Francisco, Calif. 94102-4582
(415) 863-8800

1990 Exhibitions
Thru Jan. 21
John Gutmann: Beyond the Document
Features vintage prints by the highly regarded German photographer living in San Francisco.

Thru Feb. 4
†*Bay Area Figurative Art, 1950–1965*
A definitive look at the postwar expressionist impulse as manifested on the West Coast, with works by Bischoff, Brown, Diebenkorn, Neri, Oliveira, Park. Catalogue.

Thru Apr. 15
Paul Klee: Faces & Figures
Explores Klee's representation of the human figure.

San Francisco, Calif.

Jan. 12–Mar. 11
Graciela Iturbide: Photographs of Women
Images of the Indian women of Juchitàn by the contemporary Mexican photographer.

Feb. 1–Apr. 1
Charles and Ray Eames
Illustrates step-by-step the creation of a chair by the noted furniture design team.

Feb. 2–Apr. 1
Lee Miller
Surveys the career of the talented photographer.

Mar. 1–Apr. 22
The New Vision: Photography between the World Wars
Celebrates the 150th anniversary of photography with 115 vintage images illustrating the photographic revolution in 20th-century vision in Europe and America. Includes works by Abbott, Bayer, Brancusi, Bourke-White, Cartier-Bresson, Evans, Magritte, Man Ray, Rodchenko, Stieglitz, Weston. Catalogue.

Mar. 1–Apr. 29
Morphosis: Three Houses
Features the experimental work of Los Angeles architects Thom Mayne and Michael Rotondi.

Mar. 15–May 13
Bay Area Media
Surveys aesthetic developments and technological advancements in the media arts by San Francisco Bay Area artists.

May 15–July 8
The Terrible Uncertainty of the Thing Described
Video installation presents nature in a state of turmoil accompanied by audio tracks and a Tesla coil that periodically sends bolts of low-level electricity arching across the gallery.

June 14–Aug. 26
Visionary San Francisco
Examines the development of San Francisco architecture.

June 22–Aug. 19
Minor White: In Context
An exhibition complementing the White retrospective; features the work of a diverse group of photographers influenced by White.

June 22–Aug. 19
Minor White: The Eye That Shapes
The first major retrospective of photographs by the noted American modernist.

July 10–Oct. 21
Clyfford Still: Works by the major abstract expressionist

Ein Man Versinkt vor der Krone, 1904, by Paul Klee. San Francisco Museum of Modern Art.

San Marino, Calif.

Aug. 31–Oct. 28
Grossman & Levenstein
Features the work of the contemporary photographers.

Oct. 4–Dec. 2
SECA Art Award
Presents the work of the 1990 winner of the Society for the Encouragement of Contemporary Art Award.

Oct. 11–Dec. 9
Sebastiao Salgado
Major retrospective of the South American photographer whose work reflects a fascination with ritual and mystery.

Nov. 9–Jan. 6, 1991
John Heartfield

Nov. 15–Jan. 13, 1991
Sigmar Polke
Retrospective of the German painter's work since 1963.

Dec. 20–Feb. 10, 1991
Florence Henri
Images by one of France's most important photographers.

Permanent Collection
Twentieth-century works of international scope in diverse media. **Highlights:** Gorky, *Enigmatic Combat;* Matisse, *The Girl with Green Eyes;* Pollock, *Guardians of the Secret;* Rauschenberg, *Collection;* Rivera, *The Flower Carrier;* Tanguy, *Second Thoughts;* paintings by Bay Area artists Diebenkorn, Neri, Oliveira, Thiebaud; exceptional selection of photographs by Adams, Stieglitz, Weston.

Admission
Adults $3.50; seniors & children, 6–15, $1.50; children under 6 free. Thurs., 5–9, adults $2; seniors & children, 6–15, $1. Tues., 10–5, free. Handicapped accessible.

Hours
Tues.–Wed. & Fri., 10–5; Thurs., 10–9; Sat.–Sun., 11–5. Closed Mon., Jan. 1, Thanksgiving, Dec. 25.

The Huntington

Library, Art Collections, and Botanical Gardens
1151 Oxford Rd., San Marino, Calif. 91108
(818) 405-2100

1990 Exhibitions
Thru Feb. 25 (Huntington Gallery)
Wedgwood Majolica from the Kadison Collection
Features a little-known ware style popular during the second half of the 19th century.

San Marino, Calif.

Jan. 9–May 6 (Scott Gallery)
American Landscape Drawings from the Maurice Bloch Collection
Displays works from the late 18th through 19th centuries.

Feb. 9–May 20 (Library Exhibition Hall)
Turning the Wheel Uphill: The Rise of Machinery, 1450–1800
Rare books and manuscripts trace technological advances.

Spring (Huntington Gallery)
Rustic Life in Victorian Britain: Watercolors of William Henry Hunt
Comprehensive exhibit of the 19th-century artist's work.

Summer (Scott Gallery)
Celebrating Yosemite
Commemorates the centennial of Yosemite's founding as a national park through drawings, prints, and photographs. A related exhibit is displayed concurrently in the library.

Summer (Library Exhibition Hall)
Yosemite National Park: A Centennial Celebration

Summer-Fall (Huntington Gallery)
Prints of Piranesi

Fall–Winter (Library Exhibition Hall)
Fiber to Sheet: Papermaking East and West
A library exhibit tracing the history of papermaking.

St. Anthony Reading, 1519, by Albrecht Dürer. The Huntington Library.

Permanent Collection
Library collection of rare books, manuscripts from the 11th-century to the present; renaissance paintings and bronzes; important 17th-century works by Claude Lorrain, Rembrandt, Van Dyke; 18th-century French paintings by Boucher, Nattier, Watteau; British 18th- and 19th-century painting; European decorative arts; 18th- to 20th-century American art by Cassatt, Copley, Hopper, Sargent, Sloan; European decorative arts. **Highlights:** Cassatt, *Breakfast in Bed;* Church, *Chimborazo;* Constable, *View on the Stour;* Gainsborough, *The Blue Boy;* Hopper, *The Long Leg;* Lawrence, *Pinkie;* Rembrandt, *Lady with a Plume;* van der Weyden, *Madonna and Child;* Gutenberg Bible; Chaucer's *Canterbury Tales;* early editions of Shakespeare; letters and papers of the Founding Fathers; botanical gardens including the Japanese, Desert, Rose, and Jungle gardens. **Architecture:** 1909–11 Huntington mansion by Hunt and Grey; 1984 Scott Gallery of American Art by Warner and Grey.

Admission
Donation suggested: $2. Handicapped accessible.

Hours
Tues.–Sun., 1–4:30; Sun., reservations required. Closed Mon. & holidays.

115

Santa Fe, N.M.

Tours
Garden tours, Tues.–Sat., at 1. For group tour reservations call (818) 405-2127.

Food & Drink
Patio Restaurant: Tues.–Sun., 1–4.

Museum of New Mexico

**Museum of Fine Arts
West Palace Ave., on the Plaza,
Santa Fe, N.M. 87501
(505) 827-4455**

Exterior, Museum of Fine Arts, Santa Fe, New Mexico.

1990 Exhibitions
Thru Feb. 28
Will Shuster: A Santa Fe Legend
A retrospective of the career of the colorful Santa Fe artist.

Thru Apr. 22
The Collector's Eye
Two concurrent photographic exhibitions celebrating the 150th anniversary of the medium. Selection from 25 private New Mexico collections.

Jan. 26–June 17
Sources and Inspirations: Paintings by Paul Pletka
Features realistic paintings in which the contemporary Santa Fe artist examines Native American and Hispanic traditions.

Mar. 3–July 29
The Alcove Show: Four Contemporary Artists

May 19–Sept. 16
Masterpieces of the American West: The Anschutz Collection
Traces the history of western American art.

Permanent Collection
Twentieth-century American art, primarily by artists working in the Southwest; extensive holdings of American Indian art, including work by New Mexico Indians.
Architecture: 1917 building patterned after New Mexico mission churches.

Admission
Adults $3.50; children under 17 free.

Hours
Jan.–Feb., Tues.–Sun., 10–5; Mar.–Dec., daily, 10–5.

Tours
Call (505) 827-4455 for information.

Museum of New Mexico Branches

Museum of Indian Arts and Culture
710 Camino Lejo, Santa Fe, N.M. 87501
(505) 827-8941

Museum of International Folk Art
706 Camino Lejo, Santa Fe, N.M. 87501
(505) 827-8350

The Palace of Governors
West Palace Ave., on the Plaza, Santa Fe, N.M. 87501
(505) 827-6483

Other Collections of Note

The Wheelright Museum of the American Indian
704 Camino Lejo, Santa Fe, N.M. 87501
(505) 982-4636

The John and Mable Ringling Museum of Art

5401 Bay Shore Rd., Sarasota, Fla. 34243
(813) 355-5101

1990 Exhibitions
Thru Feb. 11
†*Worthington Whittredge*
Paintings of the Hudson River school artist reveal the evolution of his career and reflect the course of American landscape painting. Catalogue.

Thru Feb. 11
Projects 4: Izhar Patkin

Feb. 20
Reinstallation of Permanent Collection

Mar. 9–May 13
Projects 5: Jeff Koons

Summer
Featuring Florida 3
Annual exhibition featuring works in a variety of media by contemporary artists from Florida.

Permanent Collection
European Renaissance and rococo paintings; baroque; antiquities, decorative arts, tapestries, photographs, drawings, prints; modern and contemporary art; circus costumes, wagons, props, and a complete scale model miniature circus;

Seattle, Wash.

circus-related fine art and memorabilia. Evolution of sculpture is traced through full-sized reproductions in the Italian Renaissance-style courtyard. **Highlights:** French, Dutch, Flemish, Spanish baroque works. **Architecture:** 1924–26 Venetian Gothic Ringling residence. Ca' d'Zan; 1927–29 Renaissance-style villa museum; 1966 addition.

Admission
Adults $6; children, 6–12, $1.75; Florida teachers, & students with valid ID, children under six free; group rates available. Handicapped accessible.

Hours
Daily, 10–6; Thurs., 10–10. Closed Jan. 1, Thanksgiving, Dec. 25.

Tours
Call (813) 355-5101 for information.

Food & Drink
Pavilion Restaurant: Open during museum hours.

Seattle Art Museum

Volunteer Park, Seattle, Wash. 98112
(206) 625-8900; 625-8901 (recorded)

1990 Exhibitions
Thru Mar. 4
Preserving an Architectural Heritage: Frank Lloyd Wright Decorative Arts
Features 70 objects including furniture, windows, metalwork, ceramics, textiles.

Jan. 18–Mar. 25
Documents Northwest: The PONCHO Series: Off the Ground: The Early Residential Works of Robert Reichert and Mark Millett

Mar. 22–May 13
Against Nature: Japanese Art in the Eighties
Contemporary installations by Funakoshi, Hirabayashi, Maemoto, Miyajima, Morimura, Ogino, Ohtake, and Yamamoto.

June–Aug.
Treasures from Moscow and the Kremlin
Focuses on 14th-century icons, illuminated manuscripts, arms and armor, textiles, paintings.

Permanent Collection
Egyptian, Mesopotamian, Greek, Etruscan, Iranian, and Islamic sculptures, ceramics, metalworks, paintings; Japanese, Chinese, East Indian, Pakistani, Southeast Asian arts; African, Oceanic, Native American art; European paintings, prints, drawings, sculptures since the 14th century; European decorative art; American paintings, sculptures, photographs

since the late 19th century; 20th-century art of the Northwest. **Highlights:** Classical coins; 18th-century European porcelain; Chinese jades and snuff boxes. **Architecture:** 1930s art deco building by Gould; 1991 downtown museum by Venturi planned.

Admission
Adults $2; seniors & students $1; children under 6 accompanied by adult free. Thurs., free. Handicapped accessible.

Hours
Tues.–Sat., 10–5; Thurs., 10–9; Sun., noon–5. Closed Mon. & holidays.

Tours
Tues.–Sun. at 2. Call (206) 625-8969.

Other Collections of Note

Henry Art Gallery
15th Ave. N.E. and N.E. 41st St.,
Seattle, Wash. 98195
(206) 543-2280

Stanford University Museum of Art

Lomita Dr. & Museum Way, Stanford, Calif.
94305-5060
(415) 723-4177

1990 Exhibitions
Thru Feb. 4
Bourke-White: A Retrospective
Features 120 works appearing in magazines *Life* and *Fortune* by the master photographer.

Jan. 9–Mar. 11
Abstraction/Representation: Sean Scully/Donald Sultan

Feb. 20–May 6
Between the Thunder and the Rain: The Final Five Generations of Traditional Chinese Painting

Mar. 20–June 17
Barbara Morgan–Photographs

May 20–June 17
Master of Fine Arts Exhibition

Summer
Asian Textiles from the Stanford Museum

Window, 1967, by Richard Diebenkorn. Stanford University Museum of Art.

Toledo, Ohio

Permanent Collection
Ancient art from Egypt, Greece, Rome; Asian, Pre-Colubian, African, North American Indian, Melanesian art; Western art since the 14th century. **Highlights:** Eighteenth- and 19th-century paintings, drawings, prints by Delacroix, Géricault, Reynolds, Turner, West, Whistler; Chinese paintings from the Ming dynasty; Cantor collection of Rodins; sculpture garden. **Architecture:** 1894 neoclassical building, modeled after the National Museum in Athens, by Percy.

Admission
Free. Handicapped accessible.

Hours
Tues.–Fri., 10–5; Sat.–Sun., 1–5. Closed Mon., holidays, & mid-Aug.–late Sept.

Tours
Available Mon.–Thurs., 8:30–4; Fri., 8:30–noon. Call (415) 723-3469.

The Toledo Museum of Art
2445 Monroe St., Toledo, Ohio 43620
(419) 255-8000

1990 Exhibitions
The West wing of the museum (European, Asian, African collections) will be closed for renovation during 1990.

Thru Mar. 25
Baroque Revisited

Jan. 13–June 3
A Page in Time: Treasured Books from the Toledo Museum of Art Collection
Features 80 examples of the art of the book from the 15th century to the present.

Jan. 27–Apr. 29
Meryon's Paris: Prints and Drawings from the Toledo Museum of Art Collection

Apr. 29–June 24
†The Romance of the Taj Mahal
Presents the world-famous monument through models, prints, drawings, and paintings by Indian and British artists; also includes gems, jewelry, carpets, textiles. Catalogue.

May 5–July 1
Like a One-Eyed Cat: Photographs by Lee Friedlander, 1956–1987
Surveys the career of the American artist whose black-and-white and unmanipulated work depicts street scenes in an experimental manner. Catalogue.

Statue of a Roman Officer, 130 A.D., Roman. The Toledo Museum of Art.

Washington, D.C.

July 14–Sept. 16
Mothers and Daughters, That Special Quality, An Exploration in Photographs

Sept. 30–Nov. 25
†Impressionism: Selections from Five American Museums
Features 85 paintings and sculptures by the celebrated impressionists and postimpressionists Bonnard, Cassatt, Degas, van Gogh, Manet, Monet, Pissarro, Renoir.

Oct. 27–Dec. 30
Early American Photography: The First Fifty Years
A comprehensive showing of works by the 19th-century pioneers of American photography. Catalogue.

Permanent Collection
Traces the history of art from ancient Egypt to the present: European and American paintings and sculptures; extensive glass collection; graphic arts; photographs; tapestries; decorative arts. **Highlights:** Chase, *The Open-Air Breakfast;* Cole, *The Architect's Dream;* El Greco, *Agony in the Garden;* Rembrandt, *Man in a Fur-Lined Coat;* Rubens, *The Crowning of Saint Catherine.* **Architecture:** 1912 classical building by Green.

Admission
Donation suggested. Entrance fee for selected exhibitions. Handicapped accessible; wheelchairs and strollers available.

Hours
Tues.–Sat., 10–4; Sun., 1–5. Closed Mon. & holidays.

Tours
Call (419) 255-8000 for information.

Food & Drink
Museum Café: Tues.–Fri. 10–2.

Arthur M. Sackler Gallery

**Smithsonian Institution, 1050 Independence Ave. S.W., Washington, D.C. 20560
(202) 357-2700**

1990 Exhibitions
Indefinite
Monsters, Myths, and Minerals
Reflects the vitality of animal imagery in Chinese art and myth; includes objects from the Han dynasty.

Thru Mar. 31
The Noble Path: Buddhist Art of South Asia
The changing imagery of Buddhism is presented in this exhibition of more than 100 objects from the Los Angeles County Museum of Art.

Washington, D.C.

Pavilions and Immortal Mountains, 1712, China. Arthur M. Sackler Gallery.

Thru Apr. 30
Along the Ganges: Photographs by Raghubir Singh

Spring
Yokohama Prints
Eighty woodblock prints chronicle the development of Yokohama, 1860–1872.

Permanent Collection
Represents many different Asian cultures and includes jades, metalwork, ceramics, lacquerware, paintings, manuscripts. **Highlights:** Chu Silk Manuscript; Sasanian rhyton; Shang dynasty bells; Ming dynasty masterpieces; Chinese decorative art; ancient Near Eastern silver and gold. **Architecture:** 1987; part of a three-story underground museum complex by Carlhian of Shepley, Bulfinch, Richardson, and Abbott.

Admission
Free. Handicapped accessible.

Hours
Daily, 10–5:30. Extended summer hours determined annually. Closed Dec. 25.

Tours
Daily. Call (202) 357-4886, Mon.–Fri.

The Corcoran Gallery of Art

**17th St. & New York Ave. N.W., Washington, D.C. 20006
(202) 638-3211; 638-1439 (recorded)**

1990 Exhibitions
Thru Mar. 26
Antoine-Louis Bayre, The Corcoran Colletion

Jan. 13–Mar. 26
Black Photographers Bear Witness: 100 Years of Social Protest

Jan. 13–Mar. 26
Facing History: The Image of the Black in American Art
Examines how social and cultural attitudes and historic events affected artists' representations of black society, 1750–1930; includes work by Benton, Copley, Eakins, Homer, Johnson, Mount, Sargent, Wood.

Feb. 3–Apr. 1
Like a One-Eyed Cat: Photographs by Lee Friedlander, 1956–1987
Surveys the career of the American artist whose black-and-white and unmanipulated work depicts street scenes in an experimental manner. Catalogue.

Washington, D.C.

Feb. 3–Apr. 8
Gallery One: Six Sculptors–The Resonance of the Odd Object

Apr. 21–June 24
10 + 10: Contemporary Soviet and American Painters
Works representing the new avant-garde in the Soviet Union and America.

May 5–June 29
Gallery One: A Study in Scale

May 6–June 29
Terra Sancta: Landscape Photographs

Permanent Collection
American art and photography, from pre-Revolutionary portraits to contemporary works; 17th-century Dutch art; 19th-century Barbizon and impressionist painting; American sculpture by French, Powers, Remington, Saint-Gaudens.
Highlights: Bellows, *Forty-two Kids;* Bierstadt, *Mount Corcoran;* Church, *Niagara Falls;* Cole, *The Departure* and *The Return;* Eakins, *The Pathetic Song;* Glackens, *Luxembourg Gardens;* Homer, *A Light on the Sea;* Morse, *The Old House of Representatives;* Powers, *The Greek Slave;* Sargent, *Mrs. Henry White;* Smibert, *Peter Faneuil.*
Architecture: 1897 beaux-arts building by Flagg; 1927 Clark Wing by Platt; 1927 addition contains the 18th-century Grand Salon from the Hôtel d'Orsay in Paris.

Admission
Free. Entrance fee for selected exhibitions: Adults $3; seniors & students $1.50. Handicapped accessible.

Hours
Tues.–Sun., 10–4:30; Thurs., 10–9. Closed Mon., Jan. 1, Dec. 25.

Tours
Call (202) 638-1070.

Head of a Negro, 1777–78, by John Singleton Copley. From *Facing History: The Image of the Black in American Art* at the Corcoran Gallery of Art, Jan. 13–Mar. 25.

Hirshhorn Museum and Sculpture Garden

Smithsonian Institution, Independence Ave. at Eighth St. S.W., Washington, D.C. 20560
(202) 357-2700

1990 Exhibitions
Thru Jan. 7
†*Francis Bacon*
Surveys the achievement of the contemporary British painter, from his daring figure studies of the 1940s to very recent, vigorously inventive works. Catalogue.

Washington, D.C.

Thru Feb. 11
Directions: Susana Solano
Large-scale architectonic sculptures by the Spanish artist.

Thru Mar. 11
Matt Mullican WORKS
An installation of a temporary, logolike rug designed for the museum's balcony room by the New York-based artist.

Feb. 8–May 6
Culture and Commentary: An Eighties Perspective
Includes artists Anderson, Clemente, Fritsch, Holzer, Koons, Levine, Schnabel, Sherman. Catalogue.

Mar. 7–June 3
Directions: Ilya Kabakov
Features an installation of several room like environments by the contemporary Soviet artist.

June 13–Sept. 9
†*Bay Area Figurative Art, 1950–1965*
A definitive look at the postwar expressionist impulse as manifested on the West Coast, with works by Bischoff, Brown, Diebenkorn, Neri, Oliveira, Park. Catalogue.

July 25–Oct. 28
David Ireland WORKS
Features a site-specific project by the San Francisco artist known for his exploration of architectural environments.

Oct. 16–Jan. 6, 1991
John Baldessari
A career survey of works by the influential Los Angeles artist-photographer, including his multilayered, postmodern narratives of image and text. Catalogue.

The Sorceress, 1961, by Jean Tinguely. Hirshhorn Museum and Sculpture Garden.

Permanent Collection
Comprehensive holdings of modern sculptures, paintings, drawings; largest U.S. public collection of sculpture by Moore; works by Hepworth, Oldenburg, Rickey, and di Suvero displayed in the sculpture garden and plaza; 19th- to 20th-century American paintings and works on paper; European and Latin masters. **Highlights:** De Kooning, *Queen of Hearts;* Eakins, *Mrs. Thomas Eakins;* Golub, *Four Black Men;* Kiefer, *The Book;* Manzu, *Cardinal;* Matisse, *Four Backs;* Moore, *King and Queen;* Rodin, *Monument to Balzac* and *Burghers of Calais;* outstanding group of Smiths; Stella, *Quaqua! Attaccati la! 4x;* sculpture garden. **Architecture:** 1974 building by Bunshaft of Skidmore, Owings, and Merrill; 1981 sculpture garden renovation by Collins

Admission
Free. Handicapped accessible.

Hours
Daily, 10–5:30; sculpture garden, daily, 7:30–dusk. Summer hours determined annually. Closed Dec. 25.

Washington, D.C.

Tours
Mon.–Sat. at 10:30, noon, 1:30; Sun. at 2:30, 3:30. Call (202) 357-3235.

Food & Drink
Outdoor café: Summer, 10–midafternoon.

National Gallery of Art

**Constitution Ave. at Fourth St. N.W.,
Washington, D.C. 20565
(202) 737-4215**

1990 Exhibitions
Thru Jan. 14
†*Expressionism and Modern German Painting from the Thyssen-Bornemisza Collection*
Works from the distinguished family collection focusing on the movements of the Brück, Blaue Reiter, Bauhaus, and Neue Sachlichkeit. Includes works by Kandinsky, Kirchner, and Nolde. Catalogue.

Thru Jan. 28
Frederic Edwin Church
Paintings by the important 19th-century American artist. Catalogue.

Thru Jan. 28
†*John Twachtman: Connecticut Landscapes*
Works by one of the most admired American impressionist painters, best known for the subtle and poetic qualities of his landscapes.

Thru Apr. 8
The 1980s: Prints from the Collection of Joshua P. Smith
Includes monotypes and hand-colored impressions, by Bartlett, Baselitz, Clemente, Fischl, Jacquette, Longo, Murray, Paladino, Rothenberg, Shapiro, Turrell. Catalogue.

Thru Dec. 31
Twentieth-Century Art: Selections for the Tenth Anniversary of the East Building
Reinstallation of the 20th-century collection. Catalogue.

Jan. 14–Apr. 29
Reinstallation of Bellini and Titian "Feast of the Gods"
The reinstallation of the painting in the company of works by Bellini, Giorgione, and other Venetian masters.

Jan. 28–Apr. 15
Selections and Transformations: The Art of John Marin
Examines the art of a central figure in the noted Stieglitz circle; oil paintings, watercolors, drawings, and etchings illuminate the artist's manner and methods. Catalogue.

Quappi in Rose, 1932–34, by Max Beckmann. From *Expressionism and Modern German Painting from the Thyssen-Bornemisza Collection* at the National Gallery of Art thru Jan. 14.

Washington, D.C.

Mar. 11–May 20
Rembrandt's Landscapes: Drawings and Prints

Mar. 18–June 3
Matisse in Morocco
Features the artist's work from his two Moroccan visits of 1912–13; includes paintings and drawings from the USSR's Pushkin and Hermitage museums as well as other public and private collections. Catalogue.

May 6–July 15
The Passionate Eye: Impressionist and Other Master Paintings from the Collection of Emil G. Buhrle
Catalogue.

May 6–Aug. 5
†*Masterpieces of Impressionism and Postimpressionism: The Annenberg Collection*
Formidable group of works by innovative 19th-century French artists; includes paintings by Cézanne, Gauguin, van Gogh, Monet, Renoir.

May 20–July 29
The Drawings of Jasper Johns
Includes landscapes, maps, flags, portraits, figures, and still lifes in a variety of media. Catalogue.

May 27–Sept. 3
Edvard Munch: Master Prints from the Epstein Family Collection
Ninety-four woodcuts and lithographs from the largest and finest private Munch collection. Catalogue.

July 1–Nov. 4
The Sculpture of Indonesia
Extraordinary exhibit of 120 works from the Neolithic period to the 13th century, including stone and bronze sculptures, metalwork, and works from 9th-century Borobudur in Java. Catalogue.

July 15–Sept. 30
George Caleb Bingham
Focuses on the artist's great genre paintings. First major exhibition of his work in more that 20 years. Catalogue.

Nov. 11–Feb. 24, 1991
Anthony Van Dyck: Paintings in the Grand Manner
Commemorates the 350th anniversary of the artist's death with some 90 portraits and religious and mythological paintings. Catalogue.

Dec. 2–Mar. 17, 1991
The Art of Glass: Twelve Centuries of European Glassmaking from the Corning Museum
Features over 100 objects of various sizes, shapes, colors, and ornamentation created for both utilitarian and decorative purposes. Catalogue.

Permanent Collection
Focuses mainly on European and American art of diverse media: Paintings, sculptures, drawings, prints, decorative art, from the 13th to 20th century, including Kress collection of Renaissance and baroque paintings, Netherlandish painting from the Golden Age, French impressionist and postimpressionist paintings, modern works. **Highlights:** Calder, *Untitled;* Miró, *Woman;* Moore, *Knife Edge Mirror;* Motherwell, *Reconciliation Elegy;* Rembrandt Peale, *Rubens Peale with a Geranium;* Picasso, *Family of Saltimbanques;* Pollock, *Number 1, 1950;* Raphael, *Alba Madonna* and *Saint George and the Dragon;* Rembrandt, *Self-Portrait;* Titian, *Venus with a Mirror;* the only painting by da Vinci in this country: *Ginevra de'Benci;* Whistler, *White Girl.*
Architecture: 1937 West Building by Pope; 1978 East Building by Pei.

Admission
Free. Handicapped accessible; wheelchairs available.

Hours
Mon.–Sat., 10–5; Sun., noon–9. Extended spring & summer hours determined annually. Closed Jan. 1 & Dec. 25.

Tours
Call (202) 737-4215 for information.

Food & Drink
Terrace Café: Mon.–Sat., 11–4; Sun., noon–4. Concourse Buffet: Mon.–Sat., 10–4; Sun., noon–6. Cascade Café: Mon.–Sat., 11–4:30; Sun., noon–3:30. Garden Café: Mon.–Sat., 11–4:30; Sun., noon–7.

National Museum of African Art

**Smithsonian Institution, 950 Independence Ave. S.W., Washington, D.C. 20560
(202) 357-4600, Mon.–Fri.; 357-2700, Sat.–Sun.**

1990 Exhibitions
Thru Jan. 4
The Essential Gourd

Thru Jan. 28
Bernard Plossu: The African Desert
Features 60 images by the French-born photographer, capturing the immensity of the African space.

Thru Sept. 3
†*Icons: Ideals and Power in the Art of Africa*
Focuses on five fundamental and recurrent themes: the male and female couple, the woman and child, the forceful male, the rider, and the outsider/stranger.

Washington, D.C.

May 11–Aug. 26
Yoruba: Nine Centuries of African Art and Thought
Explores the dynamic history and contemporary vitality of the Yoruba people of Nigeria; features about 100 objects in various media, including 17 significant works from museums in Ife and Lagos.

Permanent Collection
A comprehensive introduction to the numerous visual traditions of Africa south of the Sahara: Carved wood, ivory, modeled clay, and forged- or cast-metal works, including masks, shrines, jewelry, textiles, figures, and everyday household objects mostly from the late 19th and 20th century. **Highlights:** Extensive photograph collection. **Architecture:** 1987; part of a three-story underground museum complex by Yoshimura with Carlhian of Shepley, Bulfinch, Richardson, and Abbott.

Admission
Free. Handicapped accessible.

Hours
Daily, 10–5:30. Closed Dec. 25.

Tours
Call (202) 357-4860, Mon.–Fri.

Buffalo Grain Elevators, 1937, by Ralston Crawford. National Museum of American Art.

National Museum of American Art

Smithsonian Institution, Eighth & G Sts. N.W., Washington, D.C. 20560
(202) 357-2700

1990 Exhibitions

Thru Feb. 11
The Patricia and Phillip Frost Collection: American Abstraction, 1930–1945
Includes works by Albers, Bolotowsky, Hofmann, Moholy-Nagy, Reinhardt, and Holty, members of the American Abstract Artists group formed in 1937. Catalogue.

Thru Feb. 11
Training the Hand and Eye: American Drawings from the Cooper-Hewitt Museum

Thru Feb. 19
Treasures of American Folk Art from the Abby Aldrich Rockefeller Folk Art Center
Features 18th- to 19th-century folk art objects including paintings, fraktur, trade and shop signs, weather vanes, toys, decoys, quilts, coverlets. Catalogue.

Washington, D.C.

Mar. 30–Aug. 19
Irving Penn Master Images
Honors the photographer's gift of 120 images. Catalogue.

Apr. 6–July 29
Albert Pinkham Ryder
Includes 78 paintings of intimate landscapes and pastoral themes, rare decorative objects on gilded leather and mahogany panels, Near Eastern subjects, early marine paintings. Catalogue.

June 8–Aug. 19
George Caleb Bingham Drawings

Sept. 7–Nov. 12
Visual Poetry: The Drawings of Joseph Stella
Sixty works on paper offer insights into the romantic, symbolist, and mystical aspects of Stella's creative expression. Catalogue.

Sept. 23–Jan. 21, 1991
American Folk: The Herbert Waide Hemphill, Jr., Collection at the NMAA
Catalogue.

Oct. 5–Jan. 6, 1991
Childe Hassam: An Island Garden Revisited
First major exhibition to focus solely on the artist's impressionist paintings of the Isles of Shoals. Includes oils, watercolors, pastels. Catalogue.

Permanent Collection
Comprehensive holdings of American painting, sculpture, folk art, photography, graphic art from the 18th century to the present. **Highlights:** Works by American impressionists Cassatt and Twachtman; Moran, *Grand Canyon of the Yellowstone;* largest group of Ryder paintings; Stuart, *Portrait of John Adams;* works from the depression era; miniature portrait paintings; 20th-century folk art; Catlin's Indian paintings; Lincoln's Inaugural Reception Room. **Architecture:** 1836 Old Patent Office by Elliot and Mills; 1867 wings by Walter and Clark. Building also houses the Archives of American Art and National Portrait Gallery.

Admission
Free. Handicapped accessible.

Hours
Daily, 10–5:30. Closed Dec. 25.

Tours
Mon.–Fri. at noon; Sat. & Sun. at 2. For group tour reservations call (202) 357-3111.

Food & Drink
Patent Pending Café: Mon.–Sun., 11–3:30.

Washington, D.C.

National Museum of Women in the Arts

**1250 New York Ave. N.W., Washington, D.C. 20005-3920
(202) 783-5000**

1990 Exhibitions
Thru Jan. 7
The Book as Art II
Includes book-objects by prominent Italian artists and one-of-a-kind books and limited editions by American artists.

Thru Jan. 7
Forefront: Cheryl Laemmle
Presents large-scale paintings of birds, decoys, monkeys, and birch-bark figures. Catalogue.

Thru Feb. 25
David and Bathsheba: Artemisia Gentileschi
Features the work of the first woman to significantly contribute to early baroque painting.

Thru Mar. 11
Rosa Bonheur: Works from American Collections

Thru Apr. 22
Works on Paper
Drawings and prints from the permanent collection by Aycock, Cassatt, O'Keeffe, Sirani, and others.

Jan. 23–Mar. 18
Forefront: Judith Shea
Enigmatic sculpture of clothing to creates three-dimensional objects as surrogates for the human form.

Breakfast of the Birds, 1934, by Gabrielle Munter. National Museum of Women in the Arts.

Apr. 6–July 4
Elizabeth Frink
Contemporary animal sculpture. Catalogue.

May 8–July 8
The State of Upstate: New York Women Artists

July 24–Sept. 9
Isabel Bishop
The artist reveals a Renaissance sensitivity for light.

Sept. 24–Jan. 6, 1991
Forefront: Joan Personette
Presents abstract and representational paintings of brilliant color and intriguing optical illusions.

Permanent Collection
More than 600 works by women from 25 countries, dating from the Renaissance to the present.   Among the earliest: Fontana, *Portrait of a Noblewoman;* Sirani, *Virgin and Child.* **Highlights:** Cassatt, *The Bath;* Kahlo, *Self-Portrait;* works by painters Chicago, de Kooning, Frankenthaler, O'Keeffe, Perry, Vigée-Lebrun; sculptor Hoffman; photographer Abbott. **Architecture:** 1907 Renaissance-revival building by Wood; 1987 renovation by Scott of Keyes, Condon, and Florance.

Admission
Donation suggested: Adults $2; seniors & students $1. Handicapped accessible; wheelchairs available.

Hours
Tues.–Sat., 10–5; Sun., noon–5. Closed Mon., Jan. 1, Thanksgiving, Dec. 25.

Tours
Call (202) 783-5000 for information.

Food & Drink
Palette Café: Tues.–Fri., 11–3.

National Portrait Gallery

**Smithsonian Institution, Eighth & F Sts. N.W., Washington D.C. 20560
(202) 357-2700**

1990 Exhibitions
Thru Jan. 15
Portraits of the American Law

Thru Jan. 28
Champions on TIME
Features portraits of major sports figures.

Washington, D.C.

Thru Apr. 1
To Color America: The Portraits of Winold Reiss
Portraits of non-white Americans painted mostly in the 1920s–30s by the German-born artist.

Thru Apr. 2
Recent Acquisitions

Mar. 30–Aug. 19
Irving Penn Master Images
Photographs given to the gallery by the artist. Catalogue.

Mar. 30–Aug. 19
Photographic Treasures from the National Portrait Gallery Collection

Apr. 5–Apr. 1991
Oliphant's Presidents: Twenty-five Years of Caricature
More than 50 cartoon drawings of presidents as well as sculptures and sketchbooks.

May 5–Nov. 1991
TIME Covers: Portraits by Robert Vickrey

June 9–Nov. 4
The Five of Hearts: An American Friendship
Studies the late 19th-century Washington circle of friends, including Clover and Henry Adams, diplomat John Hay and his wife Clara, and geologist Clarence King.

Nov. 9–Jan. 13, 1991
Old Hickory: A Life Sketch of Andrew Jackson

Permanent Collection
Paintings, sculptures, prints, drawings, and photographs of Americans who contributed to the history and development of the U.S. **Highlights:** Portrait sculptures by Davidson; Degas, *Mary Cassatt;* Meserve collection of Civil War photographs; the last photograph of Lincoln; the Hall of Presidents, including Athenaeum portraits of George and Martha Washington by Stuart. **Architecture:** 1836 Old Patent Office by Mills; 1867 wings by Walter and Clark. Building also houses the Archives of American Art and National Museum of American Art.

Admission
Free. Handicapped accessible.

Hours
Daily, 10–5:30. Closed Dec. 25.

Tours
Available Mon.–Fri., 10–3; Sat.–Sun., holidays, 11–2.
For special subject tour reservations call (202) 357-2920.

Food & Drink
Patent Pending Café: Mon.–Sun., 11–3:30

Thomas Jefferson, "Edgehill Portrait," by Gilbert Stuart. National Portrait Gallery. On view May, 1990–1992.

The Phillips Collection

**1600 21st St. N.W., Washington, D.C. 20009
(202) 387-2151; 387-0961 (recorded)**

1990 Exhibitions
Thru Feb. 25
Contemporary Painting: William Willis
Abstract paintings and works on paper by a Washington artist working in the American spiritualist tradition followed by Burchfield, O'Keeffe, and others.

Thru Feb. 25
Contemporary Sculpture: Howard Ben Tre
First solo exhibition by the artist; includes 30 cast glass and metal pieces and 10 works on paper.

Jan. 20–May 6
Picasso Loans from the Carey Walker Foundation
Surveys Picasso's middle and mature periods, 1923–63.

Feb. 17–Apr. 29
†*The Intimate Interiors of Edouard Vuillard*
Paintings from the 1890s by the postimpressionist master who was a founder of the Nabis, an offshoot of the symbolist movement. Catalogue.

Mar. 10–May 27
Outdoor Sculpture: Dorothy Dehner

Apr. 14–May 27
John Cage: New River Watercolors
Paintings by the contemporary composer and artist.

June 9–Sept. 9
Nicolas de Stael in America
Presents 95 of the Russian-born French artist's paintings including abstractions, landscapes, nudes, and still lifes.

Sept. 22–Nov. 4
The Eight at the Phillips Collection
Paintings by members of the Eight, who first exhibited together in 1908; includes works by Davies, Glackens, Henri, Lawson, Luks, Prendergast, Shinn, and Sloan.

Nov. 17–Jan. 6, 1991
Eternal Metaphors: New Art from Italy

Permanent Collection
Primarily late 19th- and early 20th-century European and American painting and sculpture, including famous impressionist and postimpressionist works; major holdings of works by Bonnard, Braque, Dove, Klee, Marin; American artists represented include Avery, Diebenkorn, Hartley, O'Keeffe, Prendergast, Rothko. **Highlights:** Bonnard, *The Palm;* Cézanne, *Self-Portrait;* Chardin, *Bowl of Plums,*

Head of a Girl, 1946, by Henri Matisse. The Phillips Collection.

Washington, D.C.

a Peach, and a Water Pitcher; Delacroix, *Paganini;* El Greco, *The Repentant Peter;* Ingres, *The Small Bather;* Klee, *Arab Song;* Picasso, *The Blue Room;* Renoir, *Luncheon of the Boating Party;* Ryder, *The Dead Bird*. **Architecture:** 1897 building and 1907 Music Room by Hornblower and Mar-shall; 1920 and 1923 additions by McKim, Mead, and White; 1960 bridge and annex by Wyeth and King; 1990 renovation by Arthur Cotton Moore Associates.

Admission
Donation suggested: Adults $5; seniors & students $2.50; children under 18 free. Handicapped accessible.

Hours
Tues.–Sat., 10–5; Sun., 2–7. Closed Mon., Jan. 1, July 4, Thanksgiving, Dec. 25.

Tours
Wed. & Sat. at 2. For group tour reservations, call (202) 387-7390. Gallery talks 1st and 3d Thurs., 12:30.

Food & Drink
Café: Tues.–Sat., 10:45–4:15; Sun., 2–6:15.

Renwick Gallery

**National Museum of American Art, Smithsonian Institution, Pennsylvania Ave. at 17th St. N.W., Washington, D.C. 20560
(202) 357-2700**

Stag Attacked by Hounds, fire screen, c. 1920, by William Hunt Diederich. Renwick Gallery.

1990 Exhibitions
Thru Mar. 4
†*Masterworks of Louis Comfort Tiffany*
Includes stained-glass windows and lamps, Favrile glassware and ceramics, jewelry, and paintings by the highly imaginative and experimental American designer. Book.

Feb. 9–June 3
George Ohr: Modern Potter (1857–1918)
Features eccentric pottery, a distinctive blending of humor and art. Book.

Apr.–Sept.
Four Calligraphers

Apr. 20–Sept. 3
Tradition and Innovation: New American Furniture

July 27–Nov. 25
Structure and Surface: Beads in Contempory American Art

Oct. 26–Feb. 10, 1991
Contemporary American Studio Jewelry

Williamstown, Mass.

Permanent Collection
Prmanent collection and temporary exhibitions focus on 20th-century American crafts. **Architecture:** 1859 Second Empire-style building by Renwick; Octagon Room and Grand Salon, restored and furnished in the styles of the 1860s and 1870s.

Admission
Free. Handicapped accessible.

Hours
Daily, 10–5:30. Closed Dec. 25.

Tours
Call (202) 357-2531.

Other Washington Collections of Note

Dumbarton Oaks Research Library and Collection
1703 32d St. N.W., (202) 342-3270

Freer Gallery of Art Smithsonian Institution
Jefferson Dr. at 12 th St. S.W., (202) 357-1300

Hillwood Museum
4155 Linnean Ave., N.W., (202) 686-5807

Library of Congress
10 First St. S.E., (202) 287-5108

Meridian House International
1630 Crescent Pl. N.W., (202) 667-6800

National Building Museum
F St. between Fourth and Fifth Sts. N.W.,
(202) 272-2448

The Textile Museum
2320 S St. N.W., (202) 667-0441

Woodrow Wilson House Museum
2340 S Street, N.W., (202) 673-4034

Sterling and Francine Clark Art Institute

225 South St., Williamstown, Mass. 01267
(413) 458-9545

1990 Exhibitions
Apr.–June
Antoine-Louis Barye: Works from the Corcoran Gallery of Art

Williamstown, Mass.

Apr. 7–July 29
Between the Rivers: Itinerant Painters between the Hudson and Connecticut
Paintings from public and private collections. Catalogue.

Aug. 4–Sept. 16
*L'Estampe Originale: A Portfolio of Nineteenth-Century French Prints from the Collection of the Brooklyn Museum

Aug. 4–Sept. 30
Illustrated Books from the Sterling and Francine Clark Art Institute Library

Sept. 22–Oct. 28
Goya Etchings: Caprichos, Desastres, Tauromaquia Disparates

Nov. 17–Jan. 13, 1991
Irish Decorative Arts from the National Museum of Ireland
Features glass, silver, textiles, and small-scale furniture of the Celtic world. Catalogue.

Permanent Collection
Old master paintings, prints, and drawings by della Francesca, Gossaert, Memling, Rembrandt, Tiepolo; distinguished holdings of French 19th-century impressionist and academic paintings and sculptures; work by Barbizon artists Corot, Millet, Troyon; English silver; American works by Cassatt, Homer, Remington, Sargent. **Highlights:** Degas, *The Ballet Dancer;* Homer, *Eastern Point, Prout's Neck;* Renoir, *Sleeping Girl with Cat;* Turner, *Rockets and Blue Lights.*

Admission
Free. Handicapped accessible.

Hours
Tues.–Sun., 10–5. Closed Mon. except holidays, Jan. 1, Thanksgiving, Dec. 25.

Tours
Tues.–Sun., July–Aug., at 3.

Williams College Museum of Art

Main St., Williamstown, Mass. 01267
(413) 597-2429

1990 Exhibitions
Thru Jan. 21
Mary Cassatt: The Color Prints
Drawings, early states, and color variations of final states from U.S. and European collections. Catalogue.

Wilmington, Del.

Thru Apr. 8
...And Gladly Teach
Paintings, sculptures, drawings, prints, and decorative arts by Barye, Copley, Eakins, Gainsborough, Rodin, and others.

Jan. 13–Apr. 8
Barbara Takenaga
Works by the Williams art professor.

Feb. 3–Apr. 15
Drawn From Tradition: American Drawings and Watercolors from the Susan and Herbert Adler Collection
More than 50 19th- and 20th-century works by Bellows, Bishop, Cassatt, Cornell, Hassam, Homer, Kent, Marsh, Sargent, Sloan, and Stella.

Oct. 6–Dec. 16
†*The Art of Maurice Brazil Prendergast*
A historic retrospective of the career of Prendergast, whose watercolor and oil paintings considerably influenced the development of early 20th-century American art.

Permanent Collection
Eighteenth- to 19th-century American art by Copley, Eakins, Harnett, Hunt, Inness, Peto, Stuart; early modern works by Demuth, Feininger, Hopper, Marin, O'Keeffe, Prendergast; contemporary works by Applebroog, de Kooning, Dine, Hofmann, Nevelson, Pearlstein, Rauschenberg, Warhol; South Asian art including Indian tenth- to 18th-century sculpture and 17th- to 19th-century Mughal paintings.
Highlights: Ninth-century Assyrian reliefs; Cambodian and Indian sculptures; works by Charles and Maurice Prendergast; self-portrait by Warhol. **Architecture:** 1846 classical-revival building by Tefft; 1983 and 1986 additions by Moore and Harper of Centerbrook Architects and Planners.

Admission
Free. Handicapped accessible.

Hours
Mon.–Sat., 10–5; Sun., 1–5. Closed Jan. 1, Thanksgiving, Dec. 25.

Tours
Call (413) 597-2429 for information.

Maternal Caress, by Mary Cassatt. From *Mary Cassatt: The Color Prints* at the Williams College Museum of Art, thru Jan. 21.

Delaware Art Museum

**2301 Kentmere Pkwy., Wilmington, Del. 19806
(302) 571-9590**

1990 Exhibitions
Thru mid-Jan.
Dolls, Toys, and Teddy Bears
Annual holiday exhibit from the Richard Wright collection.

Worcester, Mass.

Thru Feb. 11
The Art of Fantasy and Science Fiction
Features about 100 works in a variety of media by artists Christensen, Whelan, Wurts, and others.

Mar. 9–May 13
Furniture by Wendell Castle
Surveys the work of the contemporary American sculptor who challenges traditional concepts of furniture design. Catalogue.

Executive Desk #444, 1974, by Wendell Castle. From Furniture by Wendell Castle *at the Delaware Museum of Art, Mar. 9–May 13.*

Permanent Collection
American painting, 1840 to the present by Beal, Church, Davies, Doughty, Eakins, Hassam, Henri, Homer, Hopper, Pyle, Sloan, the Wyeth family, and others. Pre-Raphaelite paintings by Burne-Jones, Hunt, Millais, Rossetti, Stillman.
Architecture: 1938 Georgian-style building; 1956 addition; 1987 wing by Victorine and Samuel Homsey, Inc.

Admission
Free. Handicapped accessible.

Hours
Tues., 10–9; Wed.–Sat., 10–5; Sun., noon–5. Closed Mon., Jan. 1, Thanksgiving, Dec. 25.

Tours
Available Tues.–Sat., 10–4; Sun., 1–4. For reservations call (302) 571-9594.

Worcester Art Museum

**55 Salisbury St., Worcester, Mass. 01609-3196
(508) 799-4406**

1990 Exhibitions
Indefinite
American Miniature Portraits at the Worcester Art Museum

Thru Jan. 21
The Revenge of the Forty-seven Samurai
The series of multicolor woodblock prints illustrates one of Japan's most celebrated stories of loyalty and samurai ethics.

Thru Jan. 28
Jean Lurcat: The "Moissons" Tapestry
Displays a pivotal piece in the renaissance of tapestry making of the mid-1930s.

Jan. 13–Mar. 4
New York, New York: The City in Photographs
Focuses on life in America's most dynamic city through the eyes of leading photographers such as Feininger, Pollock, and Stieglitz.

Apr. 14–Aug. 5
An American Sampler: Folk Art from the Shelburne Museum
Foremost collection of American crafts includes quilts, coverlets, scrimshaw, decoys, carousel animals, weather vanes, whirligigs. Catalogue.

Sept. 15–Dec. 2
Wild Spirits, Strong Medicine: African Art and the Wilderness

Permanent Collection
Encompasses 50 centuries of art from East to West, antiquity to the present: Indian, Persian, Japanese, Chinese art; 17th-century Dutch paintings; American 17th- to 19th-century painting; contemporary art. **Highlights:** Anonymous, *Captain John Freake*; Cassatt, *Woman Bathing;* Copley, *John Bours;* Hokusai, *The Great Wave at Kanagawa;* Kandinsky, *Untitled;* Massys, *Rest on the Flight into Egypt;* del Sarto, *Saint John the Baptist;* Renaissance court with ten mosaics from Antioch dating from the second to sixth century; Bancroft collection of ukiyo-e prints. **Architecture:** 1898 building by Earle; 1970 Higgins Wing by the Architects Collaborative; 1983 Hiatt Wing.

Mrs. Elizabeth Freake and Baby Mary, 1671–74, 17th century, American artist unknown. Worcester Art Museum.

Admission
Adults $3.50; seniors & college students with ID $2; age 18 & under free. Sat., 10–noon, free. Handicapped accessible.

Hours
Tues.–Fri., 10–4; Sat., 10–5; Sun., 1–5. Closed Mon., Jan. 1, July 4, Thanksgiving, Dec. 25.

Tours
Call (508) 799-4406 for information.

Food & Drink
Museum Café: Tues.–Sun., 11:30–2.

The Butler Institute of American Art

524 Wick Ave., Youngstown, Ohio 44502
(216) 743-1107

1990 Exhibitions
Thru Jan. 7
Regional Artist Exhibition Program
Paintings, collages, and photographs by Bertonlini, Jaffer, and Lawton.

Thru Jan. 28
Neil Welliver
Works from the landscape painter's private collection.

Youngstown, Ohio

Thru Jan. 28
Sylvia Sleigh: An Environmental Painting
Displays a single painting relating to the artist's life.

Jan. 7–Feb. 4
Masumi Hayashi Exhibition: Tribute to the Steel Industry
Large-scale panoramic photo collages accompanied by recordings.

Jan. 21–Mar. 11
Mermories of Childhood: The Great American Quilt Festival

Feb. 3–Mar. 18
Mel Pekarsky: Recent Paintings
Mixedmedia works depict the grandeur and power of nature.

Feb. 11–Mar. 25
American Realism Abroad
Works combine modern realism with European tradition.

Feb. 11–Mar. 25
East Meets West: Chen Chi in America
Features watercolors that focus on New York City themes.

June 10–Aug. 12
Larry Rivers: Public and Private
A retrospective of public and autobiographical works convey the artist's styles during the past abstract expressionist era.

June 24–Aug. 19
Fifty-fourth National Midyear Show

Permanent Collection
Three centuries of American art with unique works by western artists Bierstadt, Higgins, Remington; marine painting by Bradford, Bricher, Lane, Moran; 20th-century art including works from the Ashcan school; Donnell Gallery of American Sports Art including works by Bellows, Curry, Grooms, Lichtenstein. **Highlights:** Grooms, *Fran Tarkenton;* Homer, *Snap the Whip;* Inness, *Hazy Morning, Montclair;* Sargent, *Mrs. Knowles and Her Children.*
Architecture: 1919 Italianate building by McKim, Mead, and White; 1987 West Wing.

Admission
Free. Entrance fee for selected exhibitions. Handicapped accessible.

Hours
Tues. & Thurs.–Sat., 11–4; Wed., 11–8; Sun., noon–4.
Closed Mon., Jan. 1, Easter, July 4, Thanksgiving, Dec. 25.

Tours
Tues.–Fri., 9–4:30. Call (216) 743-1107 for information.

Museums of Canada   Calgary, Alberta

Glenbow Museum of Art

130 9th Ave., S.E., Calgary, Alberta
Canada T2G 0P3
(403) 264-8300

1990 Exhibitions

Indefinite
Art in the Religions and Myths of Mankind

Thru Jan. 28
John Hall: The Portrait Paintings
Paintings owned and selected by portrait sitters, showing Hall's super-realistic style.

Thru Jan. 28
Paterson Ewen: Phenomena, 1971–1988
Charts the development of the Canadian painter from his early abstract style to his later landscape images.

Feb. 10–Apr. 15
Ron Moppett Retrospective
Displays paintings, sculptures, and drawings by a major contemporary Canadian artist.

Apr. 28–June 10
Lowrie Lyle Warrener
A retrospective featuring 50 paintings, prints, and theater designs, 1924–40, by the versatile Ontario artist.

Apr. 28–June 17
Kathleen Munn and Edna Tacon: New Perspectives on Modernism in Canada
Oil paintings, watercolors, drawings, and collages created in the first half of this century.

June 30–Aug. 26
Retrospective Fernand Leduc
Examines the career of a major Canadian artist, who was a member of the Montreal group Les Automatistes.

Sept. 8–Nov. 4
Dmytro Stryjec: The Man and His Art
Features portraits of Ukrainian folk heroes, landscapes, and still lifes.

Oct. 20–Dec. 9
Frances Anne Hopkins (1838–1919)
Surveys the work of an early Canadian pioneer woman who recorded the "voyageur era" of Canadian history.

Permanent Collection

Chronicles the history of western Canada and includes native Indian, Inuit, and early pioneer displays; extensive mineralogy and military history collection. **Highlights:** Life-size Indian teepee; acrylic sculpture *Aurora Borealis*; Eagle

Edmonton, Alberta

Headdress; a settler's log cabin; Canadian Pacific Railway gallery. **Architecture:** 1976 building, part of the Calgary Convention Center complex, by Dale and Associates.

Admission
Adults $2; seniors 50¢; students $1; children under 12 free. Sat., free.

Hours
Daily, 10–6.

Tours
Call (403) 264-8300 for information.

Edmonton Art Gallery

2 Sir Winston Churchill Sq., Edmonton, Alberta Canada T5J 2C1
(403) 422-6223

1990 Exhibitions

Jan. 13–Feb. 25
Dmytro Stryjec: The Man and His Art
Features portraits of Ukrainian folk heroes, landscapes, and still lifes.

Jan. 20–Mar. 4
Eighty/Twenty: One Hundred Years of the Nova Scotia College of Art and Design

Jan. 20–Mar. 18
Harold Feist
A midcareer survey spanning the years, 1975–87; features 29 abstract acrylic paintings.

Feb. 3–Mar. 18
Evergon: 1971–1987
Outsized polaroids and the influence of Victorian aesthetics merge in the work of the arcane photographer.

Mar. 5–Apr. 22
Dangerous Goods: Feminist Visual Textual Practices

Mar. 24–May 6
Lyndal Osborne
Midcareer survey of the Edmonton teacher and printmaker.

Apr. 7–June 10
Art from the Roof of the World: Tibet
Bronzes, scrolls, and utensils demonstrate Tibetan visual art.

Apr. 28–June 10
Irene Whittome

Apples, Green Cloth and Windows, 1959, by Goodridge Roberts. Edmonton Art Gallery.

June 16–July 29
Victorian Painting in the Beaverbrook Art Gallery
Features paintings by 19th-century British artists from the Fredericton, New Brunswick, collection. Catalogue.

Aug. 4–Sept. 16
Canadian Mystical Painters
Compares and contrasts the art, philosophy, and religion of five prominent Canadian painters.

Sept. 1–Oct. 28
Rafael Goldchain: Nostalgia for an Unknown Land
Features photographs of Guatemala, Mexico, and San Salvador depicting myth, corruption, and indoctrination.

Sept. 22–Oct. 28
Flat Side of the Landscape: The Emma Lake Artists' Workshops
Demonstrates the significance of the workshops in the history of Candian painting.

Nov. 10–Jan. 6, 1991
Articles of Faith
Photographs by Doug Clark.

Permanent Collection
Presents an overview of the history of Canadian art.

Admission
Adults $2; students & seniors $1; members & children under 12 free; Thurs., 4–8, free.

Hours
Mon.–Wed., 10:30–5; Thurs.–Fri., 10:30–8; Sat.–Sun. & holidays, 11–5.

Tours
Available Sept.–May.

Vancouver Art Gallery

**750 Hornby St., Vancouver, British Columbia Canada V6Z 2H7
(604) 682-4668**

1990 Exhibitions
Thru Jan. 21
B.C. Contemporary: Roland Brener

Thru Feb. 12
B.C. Contemporary: Julie Duschenes

Thru Feb. 12
B.C. Contemporary: George Sawchuk

Vancouver, B.C.

Jan. 20–Mar. 19
Jeff Wall
Includes monumental illuminated transparencies by one of Canada's most internationally recognized contemporary artists. Catalogue.

Apr. 18–June 17
B.C. Contemporary: Derek Root

May 5–June 17
Eye for I: Video Self-Portraits

May 16–July 30
Mary Kelly: Interim
Recent work by the noted American feminist artists.

June–Sept.
Emily Carr Drawings and Watercolors

June 30–Aug. 6
Celine Baril: Barcelone
A multimedia audience-interactive installation.

Aug. 15–Oct. 8
Ken Lum
Includes recent language paintings, photographic/logo pieces, and furniture sculptures.

Sept. 12–Nov. 5
Victorian Painting in the Beaverbrook Art Gallery
Features paintings by 19th-century British artists from the Fredericton, New Brunswick, collection. Catalogue.

Oct. 27–Dec. 10
Eric Cameron: Divine Comedy
Features the artist's mystical "thick paintings." Catalogue.

Nov. 14–Dec. 31
Charles John Collings
Paintings by the English-born artist (1848–1931).

Dec. 19–Feb. 11, 1991
Flat Side of the Landscape: The Emma Lake Artists' Workshops
Demonstrates the significance of the workshops in the history of Canadian painting.

Permanent Collection

Extensive holdings of paintings, sculptures, prints, videos, photographs; 19th- and 20th-century British paintings; 17th- and 18th-century English watercolors; comprehensive representation of historical Canadian painting; contemporary art. **Highlights:** Over 200 works by British Columbia artist Emily Carr; 17th-century Dutch paintings; Goya, *Disasters of War;* historical works by Couture, Fuseli, and Wright of Derby. **Architecture:** 1911 civic courthouse by Rattenbury; 1982 renovation by Erickson.

Ottawa, Ontario

Admission
Adults $2.75; seniors & students $1.25; Thurs., 5–9, free.

Hours
Mon., Wed., Fri.–Sat., 10–5; Thurs., 10–9; Sun. & holidays, noon–5; Tues., Oct.–May, closed.

Tours
Call (604)-682-4668 for information.

Food & Drink
Gallery Café: 9–6.

National Gallery of Canada

380 Sussex Dr., Ottawa, Ontario
Canada K1N 9N4
(613) 990-1985

1990 Exhibitions
Thru Feb. 4
Robert Bourdeau Photographs
Landscapes, still lifes, and other images from the early 1970s and 1980s by a foremost Canadian photographer.

Jan. 5–Feb. 25
Eric Cameron: Divine Comedy
Features the artist's mystical "thick paintings." Catalogue.

Jan. 5–Mar. 4
Ron Martin, 1971–1981
Includes the artist's famous "Black Paintings."

Jan. 11–Feb. 11
Whitney Biennial: Film and Video Program.

Feb. 16–Apr. 15
Chagall the Storyteller: Three Suites of Prints
Selection of about 142 illustrations to classic texts: Ames Mortes, the Bible, Daphnis & Chloe.

Mar. 30–May 21
Hamish Fulton: Selected Walks 1969–1989
Presents photo and text works by the British artist known for his "walks" through the Americas. Examines the Yucatán, southwest United States, and Canadian tundra and includes works representing his interest in indigenous people.

May 4–June 17
From Fontainebleau to the Louvre: French Master Drawings from the Seventeenth Century
Works by such leading French artists as Poussin and Vouet document the birth and triumph of French classicism.

Parc des Champs-de-Bataille, Quebec

June 15–Sept. 3
Emily Carr
A retrospective of 150 works.

Oct. 5–Winter
Lisette Model
Features works created while the artist was living in Vienna and Paris during the 1920s and 1930s.

Dec. 21–Feb. 10, 1991
Lucius O'Brien
Retrospective exhibition of the Canadian artist and first president of the Royal Canadian Academy of Arts.

Permanent Collection
Houses the most extensive collection of Canadian art in the world; European, Asian, Inuit, American art; international collection of contemporary art; Canadian silver; indoor garden court and water court. **Highlights:** Completely reconstructed 19th-century Rideau Convent Chapel. **Architecture:** 1988 building by Safdie.

Admission
Adults $4; seniors $3; students with ID & children under 16 free. Handicapped accessible.

Hours
Summer: Sat.–Tues., 10–5; Wed.–Fri., 10–8. Winter: Tues.–Sun., 10–6; Thurs., 10–8. Closed Mon.

Tours
For reservation and group tour information call (613) 990-3908.

Food & Drink
Restaurants: Open during museum hours.

Le Musée du Quebec

1, ave. Wolfe-Montcalm, Parc des Champs-de-Bataille, Quebec
Canada G1R 5H3
(418) 643-2150

1990 Exhibitions
Thru Jan. 28
Lionel LeMoine FitzGerald
Features works of the Canadian painter and members of the Group of Seven.

Thru Feb. 11
The Campbell Collection
Displays soup tureens and ladles.

Parc des Champs-de-Bataille, Quebec

Thru Feb. 18
Suzor-Cote, Sculptor
Collection of the noted Canadian painter and sculptor.

Thru Apr. 1
Venetian Art of the Eighteenth Century in Canadian Collections

Feb. 28–Apr. 8
André Bieler in Rural Quebec
A retrospective of the Swiss-born Canadian painter's work.

Apr. 14–May 20
Paul Hunter
An exhibition of contemporary art.

Apr. 19–June 3
Sam Tata
An exhibition of contemporary photography.

May 26–June 24
Linda Covit
Presents garden-inspired art by the Montreal artist..

June 28–Aug. 19
Cecil Buller: Modernist Printmaker
A retrospective of the Montreal artist who made important contributions to the medium of block printing with his powerful modernist style.

July 5–Aug. 26
Alfred Laliberte
Features traditional Quebec art by one of the province's most famous sculptors.

Permanent Collection
Houses a collection of more than 12,000 works.
Architecture: 1927 neoclassic style building by Lacroix; renovations and expansion under construction.

Admission
Free.

Hours
June 15–Sept. 14: daily, 10–9. Sept. 15–June 14: Tues.–Sun., 10–6; Wed., 10–10. Closed Mon.

Tours
For reservations call (418) 643-4103.

Toronto, Ontario

Art Gallery of Ontario

317 Dundas St., West, Toronto, Ontario
Canada M5T 1G4
(416) 977-0414

1990 Exhibitions

Thru Jan. 7
Permeable Border: Art of Canada and the United States, 1920–1940

Thru Jan. 14
Four Hours and Thirty-eight Minutes: Videotapes by Lisa Steele and Kim Tomczak.

Thru Mar. 11
Jacques Lipchitz: A Retrospective
First major retrospective of the work of the great cubist sculptor. Catalogue.

Feb. 9–Apr. 1
Ross Bleckner
Includes about 15 paintings reflecting the decade's preoccupations with AIDS and nuclear war.

Feb. 17–Apr. 15
Frederick H. Evans: The Desired Haven
Features photographs that capture the solemn beauty of the great English cathedrals.

Apr. 5–May 21
Selections from the AGO Inuit Collection
A two-part exhibition of prints, drawings, and sculptures drawn from the Klamer and Sarick collections.

Apr. 20–June 10
Jeff Wall
Includes monumental illuminated transparencies by one of Canada's most internationally recognized contemporary artists. Catalogue.

June 29–Sept. 3
Guido Molinari, 1951–1961: The Black and White Paintings

Permanent Collection

Masterpieces representing western art since the Renaissance; including impressionist, postimpressionist, modernist, and contemporary art. **Highlights:** Canadian historical art including works by Krieghoff, Legare, Peel, Plamondon; religious carvings and paintings; The Klamer Collection and other Inuit holdings; prints and drawings. **Architecture:** 1911 home, the Grange; 1936 expansion and Walker Memorial Sculpture Court; 1974 Henry Moore Sculpture Centre and Sam and Ayala Zacks Wing; 1977 Canadian Wing and Gallery School addition.

Draped Reclining Figure, 1952–53, by Henry Moore. Art Gallery of Ontario.

Hull, Quebec

Admission
Families $9; adults $4.50; seniors & students $2.50; members & children under 12, free; Wed., 5:30–9, free. Fri., free to seniors. Handicapped accessible.

Hours
Tues.–Sun., 11–5:30; Wed., 11–9. Closed Mon.

Tours
Call for information.

Food & Drink
Restaurant: Tues.–Sun., 12–2; Wed., 5–8. Coffee Shop: Tues.–Sun., 10:30–5.

Canadian Museum of Civilization

**100, Laurier St., Hull, Quebec Canada J8X 4H2
(819) 953-8704**

1990 Exhibition
Thru Jan. 14
King Herod's Dream
Archaological treasures from the ancient city of Caesarea.

Thru Mar. 11
The Maple Leaf Forever New: The Canadian Flag

Thru Oct. 8
Masters of the Crafts: Recipients of the Saidye Bronfman Award for Excellence in the Crafts, 1977–86

Jan. 12–Mar. 31
Oaxaca Village
A colorful hands-on exhibition.

Jan. 25–May 15
The World around Me
An overview of Inuit art, emphasizing contemporary work.

Feb. 9–Apr. 27
Seasons of Celebration
Describes the cycle of canonical and folk rituals of Canadian Orthodox Christians.

Apr. 6–Sept. 23
A Coat of Many Colours: Two Centuries of Jewish Life in Canada

Apr. 12–Aug. 15
The Bergeron Circus
A miniature circus with 3,000 pieces, including clowns, jugglers, acrobats, and animals carved by Gaston Bergeron.

Hull, Quebec

Apr. 15–May 30
Under the Big Top
Features a collection of colorful lithographed circus posters from the 1900s.

Apr. 26–June 24
Children in Twentieth–Century Photography
Color and black-and-white images capture the essence of children through a variety of techniques.

June 15–Sept. 23
ART/Artifact
Explores the difference between art and artifact by comparing how objects from Africa are displayed differently in an anthropology museum than in an art gallery.

Aug. 9–Oct. 7
International Turned Objects: Explores Woodworking

Aug. 23–Oct. 11
Facing the Gods: Himalayan Ritual Masks

Nov. 8–Apr. 1, 1991
Weather vanes

Nov. 22–Feb. 3, 1991
Costume as Communication
Examines how Latin American costumes, wearing apparel and textiles communicate cultural ideas and values.

Oct. 25–Dec. 30
Rhythms of Change: Indian Art in Transition

Oct. 26–Dec. 28
In Splendor and Seclusion
Features the cloistered women of the royal court of Benin, a portrait by the first foreign woman permitted in the court since the 19th century.

Vase, 1981, by Wayne Ngan. Canadian Museum of Civilization.

Permanent Collection
Large museum complex dedicated to presenting Canada's history and heritage. **Highlights:** Life-size reconstructions of historic sites; Children's Museum. **Architecture:** 1989 complex by Douglas Cardinal in collaboration with Tétreault, Parent, Languedoc et Associés.

Admission
Adults $4.50; seniors & students, 16–21, $3.25; members & children under 16 free. Thurs., free. Handicapped accessible.

Hours
Summer: June 30–Sept. 4, daily, 10–8. Winter: Sept. 5–May 18, daily 10–5; Thurs., 10–8. Closed Mon. & Dec. 25.

Index by Museum

Albright-Knox Art Gallery, **16**
American Craft Museum, **86**
Amon Carter Museum, **41**
Art Gallery of Ontario, **148**
The Art Institute of Chicago, **21**
The Art Museum, Princeton University, **100**
Arthur M. Sackler Gallery, **121**
Asian Art Museum of San Francisco, **109**
The Baltimore Museum of Art, **3**
The Barnes Foundation, **97**
Birmingham Museum of Art, **8**
Brandywine River Museum, **19**
The Brooklyn Museum, **13**
Buffalo Bill Historical Center, **28**
The Butler Institute of American Art, **139**
Canadian Museum of Civilization, **149**
The Carnegie, **98**
Center for the Fine Arts, Miami, **66**
The Chrysler Museum, **88**
Cincinnati Art Museum, **25**
The Cleveland Museum of Art, **27**
Columbus Museum of Art, **29**
Contemporary Arts Museum, Houston, **49**
Cooper-Hewitt Museum, **76**
The Corcoran Gallery of Art, **122**
Crocker Art Museum, **104**
Dallas Museum of Art, **31**
The Dayton Art Institute, **32**
Delaware Art Museum, **137**
Denver Art Museum, **33**
Des Moines Art Center, **35**
The Detroit Institute of Arts, **37**
The Dixon Gallery and Gardens, **64**
Dumbarton Oaks, **135**
Edmonton Art Gallery, **142**
The Fine Arts Museums of San Francisco, **110**
Freer Gallery of Art, **135**
The Frick Collection, **77**
Glenbow Museum of Art, **141**
The Grey Art Gallery and Study Center, **87**
The Harvard Art Museums, **17**
The Heard Museum, **98**
Henry Art Gallery, **119**
Herbert F. Johnson Museum of Art, **52**
The High Museum of Art, **1**
Hillwood Museum, **135**
Hirshhorn Museum and Sculpture Garden, **123**
Honolulu Academy of Arts, **47**
Hood Museum of Art, **44**
Hunter Museum of Art, **20**
The Huntington, **114**
Institute of Contemp. Art, Boston, **9**
Institute of Contemp. Art, Philadelphia, **93**
International Center of Photography, **87**
Isabella Stewart Gardner Museum, **10**
The J. B. Speed Art Museum, **62**
J. Paul Getty Museum, **63**
Jacksonville Art Museum, **53**
The Jewish Museum, **78**
The John and Mable Ringling Museum of Art, **117**
Joslyn Art Museum, **92**
Kimbell Art Museum, **42**
La Jolla Museum of Contemporary Art, **56**
Laguna Gloria Art Museum, **2**
Library of Congress, **135**
Los Angeles County Museum of Art, **58**
The Menil Collection, **50**
Meridian House International, **135**
The Metropolitan Museum of Art, **79**
Milwaukee Art Museum, **67**
The Minneapolis Institute of Arts, **69**
The Mint Museum of Art, **19**
Modern Art Museum of Fort Worth, **44**
Le Musée du Quebec, **146**
Museum of American Folk Art, **87**
Museum of Art, Fort Lauderdale, **39**
Museum of Art, Rhode Island School of Design, **101**
Museum of Contemp. Art, Chicago, **23**
Museum of Contemp. Art, Los Angeles, **61**
Museum of Fine Arts, Boston, **11**
The Museum of Fine Arts, Houston, **50**
Museum of Fine Arts, St. Petersburg, **106**
Museum of Modern Art, New York, **81**
Museum of New Mexico, **116**
National Building Museum, **135**
National Gallery of Art, **125**
National Gallery of Canada, **145**
National Museum of African Art, **127**
National Museum of American Art, **128**
National Museum of Women in the Arts, **130**
National Portrait Gallery, **131**
The Nelson-Atkins Museum of Art, **54**

Index by Museum cont'd

New Museum of Contemp. Art, **83**
New Orleans Museum of Art, **74**
Newport Harbor Art Museum, **87**
Norton Simon Museum, **93**
Oakland Museum, **91**
Oregon Art Institute, **99**
The Peale Museum, **7**
Pennsylvania Academy of the Fine Arts, **94**
Philadelphia Museum of Art, **95**
The Phillips Collection, **133**
Phoenix Art Museum, **97**
The Pierpont Morgan Library, **87**
Renwick Gallery, **134**
The Saint Louis Art Museum, **105**
San Diego Museum of Art, **108**
San Francisco Museum of Modern Art, **112**
Seattle Art Museum, **118**
Smith College Museum of Art, **189**
The Solomon R. Guggenheim Museum, **84**
Spencer Museum of Art, **57**
Stanford University Museum of Art, **119**
Sterling and Francine Clark Art Institute, **135**
Storm King Art Center, **71**
The Studio Museum in Harlem, **87**
Terra Museum of American Art, **24**
The Textile Museum, **135**
Timken Art Gallery, **109**
The Toledo Museum of Art, **120**
University Art Museum, Berkeley, **7**
University Museum of Archaeology and Anthropology, **97**
Vancouver Art Gallery, **143**
Virginia Museum of Fine Arts, **102**
Wadsworth Atheneum, **46**
Walker Art Center, **70**
The Walters Art Gallery, **5**
The Wheelright Museum of the American Indian, **117**
Whitney Museum of American Art, **85**
Williams College Museum of Art, **136**
Woodrow Wilson House Museum, **135**
Worcester Art Museum, **138**
Yale Center for British Art, **72**
Yale University Art Center, **73**

Index by State

Alabama, **8**
Arizona, **97,98**
California, **7, 56, 58–61, 63, 87, 91, 93, 104, 108–114, 119**
Colorado, **33**
Connecticut, **46, 72, 73**
Delaware, **137**
Florida, **39, 53, 66, 106, 117**
Georgia, **1**
Hawaii, **47**
Illinois, **21–24**
Iowa, **35**
Kansas, **57**
Kentucky, **62**
Louisiana, **74**
Maryland, **3–7**
Massachusetts, **9–12, 17, 18, 89, 135, 136, 138**
Michigan, **37**
Minnesota, **69, 70**
Missouri, **54, 105**
Nebraska, **92**
New Hampshire, **44**
New Jersey, **100**
New Mexico, **116, 117**
New York, **13–16, 52, 71, 76–87**
North Carolina, **19**
Ohio, **25–27, 29, 32, 120, 139**
Oregon, **99**
Pennsylvania, **19, 93–97, 98**
Rhode Island, **101**
Tennessee, **20, 64**
Texas, **2, 31, 41–44, 49,–50**
Virginia, **88, 102**
Washington, **118, 119**
Washington, D.C., **121–135**
Wisconsin, **67**
Wyoming, **28**
Canada, **141–149**

1990 TRAVELER'S GUIDE TO MUSEUM EXHIBITIONS

☐ Please send me _____ copy(ies), at $9.95 each, of the **1990 Traveler's Guide to Museum Exhibitions** (postage and handling included for 1–4 copies). Enclosed is my check for $_____.

PLEASE SHIP TO:
Name _____

Address _____

City _____ State _____ Zip _____

☐ Please reserve _____ copy(ies) of the **1991 Traveler's Guide to Museum Exhibitions.** Bill me when ready to ship.

Note: Inquire about custom publishing a special gift edition for your association or company. Write for details.

Mail this coupon with check to: Museum Guide Publications, Inc., P.O. Box 25369, 1619 31st Street, N.W., Washington, D.C. 20007.

- -

1990 TRAVELER'S GUIDE TO MUSEUM EXHIBITIONS

☐ Please send me _____ copy(ies), at $9.95 each, of the **1990 Traveler's Guide to Museum Exhibitions** (postage and handling included for 1–4 copies). Enclosed is my check for $_____.

PLEASE SHIP TO:
Name _____

Address _____

City _____ State _____ Zip _____

☐ Please reserve _____ copy(ies) of the **1991 Traveler's Guide to Museum Exhibitions.** Bill me when ready to ship.

Note: Inquire about custom publishing a special gift edition for your association or company. Write for details.

Mail this coupon with check to: Museum Guide Publications, Inc., P.O. Box 25369, 1619 31st Street, N.W., Washington, D.C. 20007.